Creating Child-Centered Materials

Judith Rothschild Stolberg and Ellen R. Daniels
Introduction by Pamela A. Coughlin
Illustrated by Jean Iker

CHILDREN'S RESOURCES INTERNATIONAL, INC.
WASHINGTON, DC

Library of Congress Catalog Card Number: 98-070234
ISBN: 1-889544-10-8

Children's Resources International, a nonprofit organization located in Washington, D.C., promotes the implementation of sound educational practices developed in the United States while maintaining the cultural traditions of the participating countries.

The Soros Foundation/Open Society Institute is a network of foundations, programs, and institutions established and supported by philanthropist George Soros to foster the development of Open Societies around the world, particularly in the former communist countries of Central and Eastern Europe and the former Soviet Union. To this end, the Step by Step program was developed as a collaborative project of the Open Society Institute, the network of Soros Foundations, Children's Resources International and the International Step by Step Association and its members.

Children's Resources International, Inc.
5039 Connecticut Ave., NW, Suite One
Washington, DC 20008
202.363.9002 phone
202.363.9550 fax
e-mail: info@crinter.com
www.childrensresources.org

Open Society Institute, New York
400 West 59th Street
New York, New York 10019
212.548.0600 phone
212.548.4679 fax
e-mail: osnews@sorosny.org

Table of Contents

Acknowledgments

George Soros' enduring commitment to open societies and his belief that even the youngest members of these societies can practice basic democratic freedoms motivated the development of this book and others in the *Creating Child-Centered Classrooms* series.

We would also like to acknowledge our appreciation for the support of Liz Lorant and Sarah Klaus at the Open Society Institute who have provided invaluable assistance and encouragement to the program. Their dedication has been one of the keys to the program's success.

The in-country teams who have implemented the Step by Step program over the past several years were the source of many of the activities presented in this book. Their preschool and primary teachers came to understand the concept of child-centered teaching and then used their creativity to develop the necessary supportive materials at low- or no-cost. We are both humbled and inspired by their dedication to creating child-centered educational experiences for children and their families despite significant political and financial obstacles.

Many individuals collaborated to produce *Creating Child-Centered Materials* and we are most thankful to them. Judy Cusick edited the manuscript. Jean Iker developed the format for the text and enlivened it with her joyful illustrations. The Crosby Group created the book cover design, which captures the "make it yourself" spirit of the book.

Each of the staff at CRI contributed to the publication of this book. Julie Empson managed the process of coordinating the work of the authors, artist, and editor with unfailing good humor, insightful advice, and determination to produce the highest quality manual for teachers and families. Kate Burke Walsh contributed the "Home Connections" and Carolyn Rutsch reviewed the manuscript drafts. Michele Redalen edited and updated this year 2000 edition. Cassie Marshall and Jamie duPont formatted the manuscript and made sure that the information was accurate and pleasing to read. We hope you enjoy it!

The authors and staff of Children's Resources International, Inc.

INTRODUCTION
CRI

Introduction

The Value of Teacher-Made Materials

Creating Child-Centered Materials, written as a companion to the *Creating Child-Centered Classrooms* series, offer teachers of children ages 3 to 6 years activities made from commonly available materials. The activities are designed to reinforce the goals of the Step by Step program: individualizing learning experiences, encouraging children to make choices, and involving families in the education of their children.

The initial inspiration for this book came from Step by Step teachers around the world who have limited selections of educational materials to equip their classrooms. Many school systems are unable to pay for expensive classroom materials, and very few open-ended materials were available for teachers to provide "hands on" learning experiences for young children, especially in the areas of science and math.

Regardless of the wealth of materials available to a classroom, there is an intrinsic value for teachers to have their own collections of professional materials for teaching. Good teaching materials are essential for learning and the supply must be ample so that children can use them liberally for experimentation. Effective teacher-made materials build on the child's unique interests and developmental needs.

The materials and activities in this book provide opportunities for active learning. Many are commercially unavailable, because they are specifically designed to serve a singular purpose or to meet an individual need. Other materials or activities are well known, and have been adapted. All are simple to make from readily available, low-cost supplies, and each activity has a "home connection" that extends the learning experience to the home.

Many commercially available teaching materials fail to include the principles of diversity and inclusion. In a natural and thoroughly integrated fashion, teacher-developed materials include representation of diverse ethnic groups, ages, genders, professions, and disabilities.

The growing need for environmental protection provides one more reason to develop teacher-made materials from recycled materials. Children, families, and teachers must consciously reduce waste and the drain on the limited supply of natural resources. Children learn lessons about protecting the environment when they use recycled materials.

The materials used here are safe for children. Both teachers and parents should be concerned with safety issues as they collect materials and develop educational activities from found objects. Glass containers should be avoided in favor of plastic. Children involved in wood working activities should use real tools rather than toy or plastic tools and wear safety goggles. The best safety precaution is adult supervision. Teachers involve family members to provide help during activities that require increased supervision.

Background of the Step by Step Program

> *"If a society values obedient followers, its educational goals and methods will be quite different from those of a society which values independent and critical thinkers."*
>
> Urie Bronfenbrenner

The primary purpose of the Step by Step program is to educate children to participate in a democratic society. Even very young children can make effective choices, understand the consequences of their actions, and respect the different styles of fellow students under the guidance of a teacher. The Step by Step program advances child-centered teaching that respects the individual learning style and developmental stages of each child.

The fundamentals of the Step by Step program include an emphasis on:

- Individualizing learning experiences for each child
- Assisting children to make choices through planned activities in activity centers
- Family participation

Individualizing

Each child is a unique combination of genetic heritage, personality, cultural and family background, and experience. The content of the curriculum, the teaching methods, the classroom materials, and the adult interaction with children should be responsive to these individual differences. Teachers individualize by respecting the present developmental stage of each child and the unique approach that each child brings to the learning experience by planning a range of appropriate activities to ensure each child's successful experience.

The child-centered classroom supports individualized learning. Thoughtful teacher planning ensures that the activities are relevant to each child. Children individualize for themselves based on their interest and skills when they choose a particular activity. By planning flexible and interesting activities and by carefully observing children during the activities, the teacher can change and adapt materials and activities as needed. Most activities are conducted in small groups to maximize the opportunities for individualization.

When children learn at their own pace, the classroom becomes a dynamic and changing environment filled with materials and experiences designed to correspond to children's individual interests and developmental stages.

Making Choices

The Step by Step classroom is arranged in activity centers to encourage children to make choices based on their interests. The activity centers contain many different materials for exploration and play. They may vary from classroom to classroom, but activity centers usually include:

Mathematics/Manipulatives	Literacy
Science	Art
Sand and Water	Outdoor Activities
Dramatic Play	Blocks
	Music

The materials in activity centers stimulate and challenge children to use all their senses. Through experimentation, investigation, and discovery, children test ideas and gain information in their own individual ways. This is how children develop the habit of solving problems, thinking critically, and making choices.

Young children should not be forced to pursue an activity that is not of interest to them. Instead, the classroom is set up to provide a choice of activities and diverse materials from which children may choose.

Family Participation

Families are the primary educators of children and have the greatest influence upon them. Consequently, in the Step by Step program, families reinforce and expand classroom learning, and the teacher builds on the interests and learning that occur at home. The reciprocity between home and school reflects a mutual respect between parents and teachers.

Step by Step is a multi-generation program. It promotes family participation in many ways: family members assist in classrooms; they are actively involved in decision-making through parent advisory committees; and they contribute information for the teaching team about the developmental needs and strengths of their children. Teachers and parents share the responsibility of working together to develop communication, mutual respect, and acceptance of differences.

The Role of the Step by Step Teacher

In child-centered classrooms, the role of the teacher shifts from imparting information to facilitating learning. The teacher guides, stimulates, shares responsibility for learning with the children, and creates a safe environment for them. She is still the adult in charge, but the emphasis is on the self-directed role of the child's learning.

The teacher facilitates learning in the following ways:

- The teacher provides a wide variety of experiences and materials to give children ample opportunity to interact with their environment. Children learn best by doing. They need to figure out how things work through trial and error. Multiple active experiences reinforce a learning concept. Children learn patterns by tapping a musical beat—tum, tum ta, tum, tum ta on a drum; by weaving alternating colors in cloth; by stringing beads in blue, yellow, blue, yellow, blue patterns.

- The teacher observes carefully how children interact with materials. This observation will give the teacher clues to activities that build on specific interests (such as trucks or animals), special needs (a child with limited vision may need to reinforce learning through tactile experience), or learning style (a very active child may be calmed by water play). Alternatively, the teacher should observe which activity centers or activities children ignore, and explore why they ignore them.

- The teacher must understand typical child growth and development in order to provide a realistic array of learning materials and activities for each child at his particular level of development.

- The teacher asks open-ended questions to help children explore and extend learning. Open-ended questions allow for more than one right answer. They also provide insight into the child's thinking process. The questioning process improves both the child's reasoning skills and language usage. In classrooms where teachers ask questions, children, too, will ask questions. The development of the thinking process has greater implications for learning than memorizing factual information.

- The teacher gives children time to reflect on their activities in order to fully understand a concept. She allows time for children to answer questions and express their ideas independently.

- The teacher discusses both accurate and inaccurate conclusions with children. Children often benefit more from discussing an idea that proves to be incorrect than from discussing one that proves to be correct.

- Like the child, the teacher actively takes risks. She is receptive to new materials and the use of familiar materials in new ways. Some activities will be more successful than others. Not every child will enjoy or participate in every activity. The teacher with initiative will substitute materials when necessary and extend the activity when it is successful. She will change an activity to encourage children to try new things.

- The teacher acknowledges that she does not know the answer, rather than give inaccurate information. By saying, "I don't know," the teacher creates an environment where she and the children are active participants in search for answers. It also shows children the value of using resources. Children learn that adults are learners too.

- The teacher interacts and plays with the children. She joins them in their sense of wonder and takes an active interest in their endeavors.

- Equally important is that the teacher knows when to withdraw and allow the children to direct their own learning.

The Teachers' Collections of Materials

Just as doctors carry their own stethoscopes with them, so teachers' collections become their personal, unique teaching tools. For children, collections are useful to either introduce or reinforce a concept being taught. They help children expand and organize experiences related to the concept. As collections grow they afford children variety, and new activities often grow out of them. Collections are often conceived as teachers see that something has captured children's interest or conversely when they are searching for a way to encourage an interest in an activity center that a child has avoided. They are also useful when teachers recognize that children need review and extension of a particular concept.

The following vignette shows how one teacher's insight formed the beginning of a collection.

> *The children were dealing with the concept of large and small in class. At home, as she folded the wash, the teacher came across a man's undershirt and minutes later a baby's small undershirt, and the idea for a collection was born. To the shirts she added a tiny pencil and a very large one, a doll's shoe and a large old sneaker, a small comb and a big one, a small coffee spoon and a large wooden cook's spoon, a small key to a child's lock and a big key to an old door.*

She placed the collection in the dramatic play area where alert children soon discovered it. As they exclaimed over it and began to use it, she encouraged discussion related to the size and use of each item. Later she brought a pencil and comb that were bigger than the original large ones, and dealt with relational concepts as a child exclaimed, "Now the large comb is the small comb!"

Just as children develop individual interests, teachers become interested in useful collections for meeting children's needs. A bridge picture collection showing many types of bridges grew in a effort to encourage a child whose bridge building had become stagnated. The teacher mounted pictures of very different bridges at eye level in the block corner in hopes that it would stimulate change. When parents saw the collection they sent post cards of bridges from towns and cities where they vacationed. The older children enjoyed finding the cities and countries on the globe.

Collections of pictures provide unlimited opportunities for learning. One teacher's collection of pictures of emotions integrated issues of diversity and provided opportunities to talk about feelings that are common to all people. A "sleep" collection gave children a way to discuss pleasant evening rituals practiced by families as well as night fears that most children have. A "What's Happening Here?" collection was a springboard for language development, imagination, and story telling.

Teachers adapt collections to the themes in the classroom, concepts that require reinforcement, and interests of the children. Collections of pair cards—children match two identical pictures mounted on cards—provide opportunities for children to expand vocabulary, recognize similarities and differences, and learn new information. Some suggestions for pair cards are as follows:

- Baby Pair Cards are useful to stimulate discussion if there is a new baby in the family. Sibling rivalry sometimes occurs as the younger child gets more attention.
- Doctor or Dentist Pair Cards provide familiarity about a visit to the doctor or dentist. If pictures are not available, perhaps a parent who draws well can develop a series for the classroom.
- Pet Pair Cards involve children who like animals.
- Transportation Pair Cards help develop an interest in transportation: cars, trains, planes, boats, carts, spacecraft, and ships pictures.
- Food Pair Cards develop knowledge of vegetables, fruits, dairy products, and so forth.
- To introduce the idea of making sets of pair cards at home, use pictures of well-known sites in the country, city, or town.

Sources for Teacher-Made Materials

A wide variety of recycled or commonly found materials are available for teachers to use in developing sound educational activities for the classroom. Every teacher should keep a "wish list" of materials she wants to collect for particular activities and elicit the help of the children and families to collect these. The wish list can be posted on the family bulletin board or sent home by flyer or newsletter. The sources include:

- the natural environment—rocks, seeds, leaves, nuts, bark, sticks
- materials from home—containers of varying sizes, jars, plastic soda bottles, cans, food coloring, wood and metal scraps, toilet paper rolls, newspapers, Styrofoam trays, cardboard cartons, bottle caps, nails, screws, fabric, food boxes, packing materials, magazines, calendars, broken small appliances
- equipment from shops and businesses—pieces of carpet, insulated wire, wood scraps, sawdust, used computer paper, discarded small appliances

The materials should be organized, labeled, and stored so that they are readily accessible to teachers.

How to Use *Creating Child-Centered Materials*

Each illustrated activity begins with a purpose that explains the educational concept for the activity and then follows with a list of materials and directions, a description of how to use the activity, a home connection that gives tips for involving family members in either the preparation or use of the activity, and extensions that suggest ways to adapt and vary the activity.

Accompanying the activity are illustrated symbols that indicate at a glance the intended age and the activity center that the activity is best suited for.

All activities in the book are designed for children between three and six years. These symbols indicate specific ages that the activity is appropriate for:

These symbols designate which activity center each activity is designed for:

Mathematics/ Manipulatives

Science

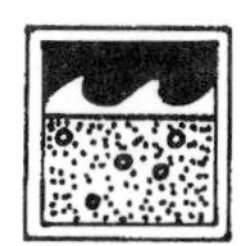
Sand and Water

Dramatic Play

Literacy

Art

Outdoor Activities

Blocks

Music

The matrix that follows identifies one or more appropriate activity centers for each activity. All of the activities support a child's growth in one or more developmental domains: social and emotional development, art, language arts, science, mathematics, physical development, and social studies.

Although the activities in the book have been used by classroom teachers, it is always prudent for teachers to practice a new activity before trying it with the children. As teachers become more experienced using child-centered methods, they will grow increasingly more comfortable creating classroom materials suited to the needs of the individuals and the group. These materials are not intended to be patterns for children to copy. Instead, they should stimulate the imagination and creativity of the children who use them.

The activities in this book were developed by teachers and used effectively in classrooms throughout the world. They are intended to be a beginning point. Be creative and build a collection of materials and activities that are right for the children you teach and share them with other teachers.

Matrix

	art	blocks	dramatic play	literacy	math/manipulatives	music	outdoor activities	sand & water	science	page number
Popstick Pockets					X					16
Bottle Caps to Dots					X					18
Number Puzzles					X					20
Same or Different Quantities					X					22
Number Lotto					X					24
Number Book				X	X					26
Butterfly Counter					X					28
Geoboard					X					30
Shape and Number Envelopes					X					32
Shape Pair Cards					X					34
Color Dominoes					X					36
Shape and Dot Dominoes					X					38
Wooden Dominoes					X					40
The Fishing Pond			X		X				X	42
Classification by Attribute Cards					X					44
Piaget's Pennies					X					48
Geometric Puzzle	X				X					50
Fruit Graph				X	X					52
Survey Graph				X	X					54
Beginners' Tangrams					X					56
Intermediate Tangrams					X					62
Advanced Tangrams					X					66
Sewing Cards and Dressing Boards	X		X		X					70
Magnets: Yes or No					X				X	74

	art	blocks	dramatic play	literacy	math/manipulatives	music	outdoor activities	sand & water	science	page number
Exploring Magnetism					X				X	76
Sink/Float								X	X	78
Measuring Liquids					X			X	X	80
Soluable Substances								X	X	82
Experiment with Sponges					X			X	X	84
Exploring with Different Size and Shape Magnets					X				X	86
Water Drop Slide									X	88
Creating Variations of Colors	X								X	90
Fizz Surprise								X	X	92
Marble Shoot									X	94
Soap Suds								X	X	98
Bubble Blowing	X						X	X	X	100
Making and Using Sieves								X	X	102
Walnut Shell Boats								X	X	104
Ordination								X	X	106
Oil and Water								X	X	108
A Visit to the Post Office		X	X							112
Tin-Can Telephones			X	X						114
Binoculars			X				X		X	116
Shadow Play			X				X		X	118
Megaphones			X				X			120
The Money Box			X		X					122
Touch-and-Tell Mystery Box				X	X				X	126
Color Flip Book				X	X					128
Lotto Boards				X	X					130
Puppets	X		X	X						132

	art	blocks	dramatic play	literacy	math/manipulatives	music	outdoor activities	sand & water	science	page number
The Important Box				X						134
A Book About Me				X						136
The Big Catch				X	X					140
Letter Cards				X						142
Seed Collage	X				X					146
Printmaking	X				X				X	148
Finger Painting	X								X	150
Patterns	X				X				X	152
See-Through Strips	X								X	154
Rubbings	X								X	156
Wax Resist	X								X	158
Box Weaving	X				X					160
Food Carton Mobiles	X				X				X	162
Making an Art Easel	X									164
Pressed Leaf Book				X			X		X	168
Outside Water Painting							X	X	X	170
Gardeners							X		X	172
Young Scientists				X			X		X	176
Adopt a Tree							X		X	178
Rivers and Bridges		X	X							182
The Hoist		X	X							184
Traffic Signs		X	X	X						186
Parking Garage		X	X							188
Discovering Equivalence		X								190
Inclined Planes		X			X		X		X	192
Sound Cans					X	X				196
Maracas	X					X				198
Kazoo	X					X				200
Wooden Harps						X			X	202
Box Banjo						X			X	204

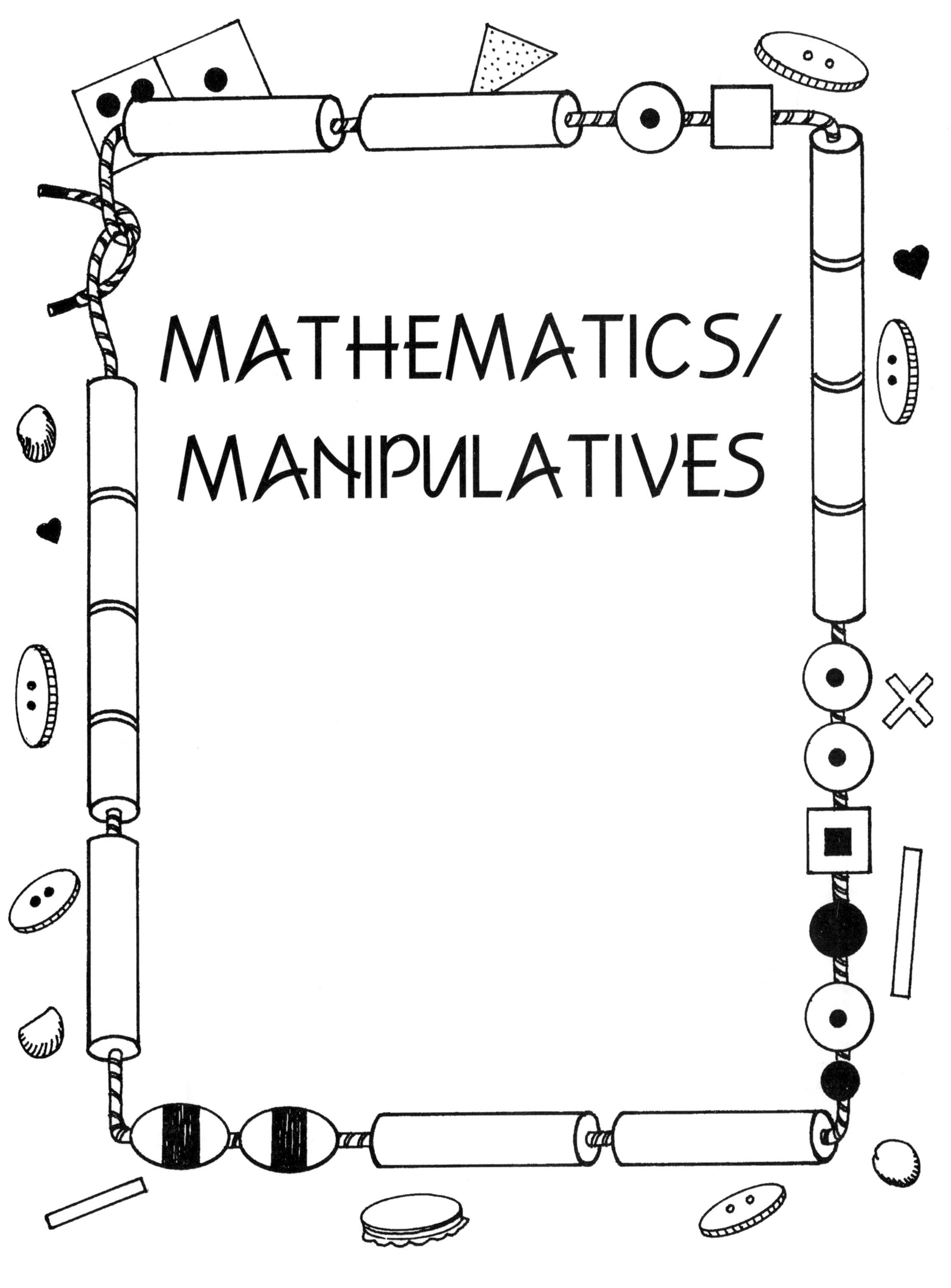
MATHEMATICS/
MANIPULATIVES

Popstick Pockets

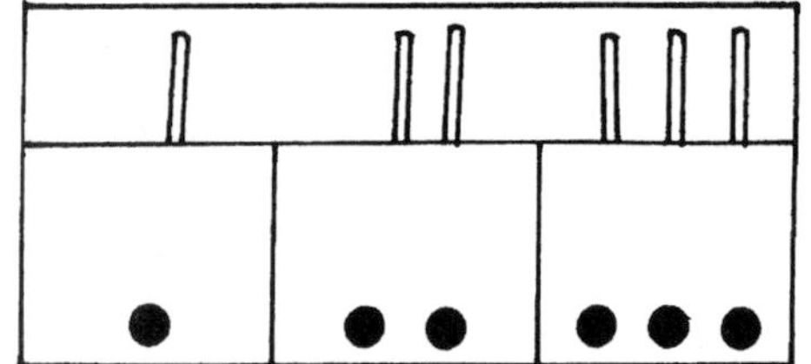

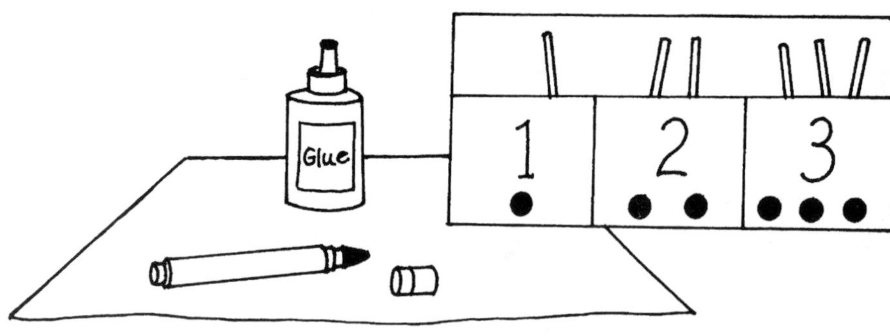

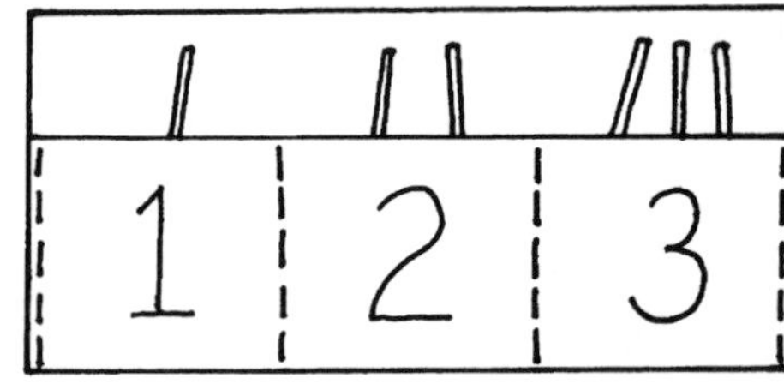

Purpose: The following 3 games are designed to give children mathematical experiences with tangible objects. They encourage the association of tangible materials with symbols and numerals. Young children can often recite numbers by rote, but not necessarily understand what they stand for. Children need time, opportunity, and many experiences handling real objects before they understand abstract numerals. This activity moves in 3 steps, from simple to slightly more complex, so that children can move at their own pace and developmental stage. The steps are prerequisites for developing a strong understanding of numbers and numeration.

HOME CONNECTION

Ask parents to save sticks for this activity. They can also help make the pockets in an informal session after school or at home in the evening if they are not free during the day. The pockets can be made of fabric by a willing parent; these are more durable for the class.

Materials:

popsticks
ruler or measuring tape
scissors
glue
thick paper

Preparation:

1. Cut out 12 dots and 2 sets of the numerals 1, 2, and 3.

2. Make 3 sets of 3-sectioned pockets out of thick paper.

3. On the first set of pockets, glue 1 dot on the left pocket, 2 dots on the middle pocket, and 3 dots on the right pocket. (Or, if a parent is making the pockets out of fabric, sew on buttons.)

4. On the second set of pockets, place 1 dot and the numeral 1 on the left pocket, 2 dots and the numeral 2 on the middle pocket, and 3 dots and the numeral 3 on the right pocket.

5. On the third set of pockets, place the numeral 1 on the left pocket, the numeral 2 on the middle pocket, and the numeral 3 on the right pocket.

Activity: In a group of 3 children, give each child a popstick pocket and several popsticks (or tongue depressors). At first, the children may just enjoy randomly putting the sticks in the pockets. Give them time to explore and discover. On their own, some will begin to associate one dot with one stick. Others may just need more time, and some may need a teacher's prompting: "How many dots do you see here? One - yes. Can you put one stick in the pocket? Good! How many dots are next? Two - yes! How many sticks go in there? Let's see you put the same number of popsticks in the last pocket as there are dots on the pocket." When the child masters the activity with dot-only pockets, introduce the dot/numeral, then the numeral pockets.

Extensions and variations:

- Make popstick pockets with numerals from 4 - 6, 7 - 9, etc.

- Make collections of pebbles, buttons, or keys in a bowl. Take 1 pebble and place it in front of you. Now ask a child to take the same amount and place it in front of her. Can she match sets and count the objects? As the child's facility with numbers increases, create more complex addition and subtraction games. How many combinations of pebbles can you think of to make 5? How many do you remove to get 3?

Bottle Caps to Dots

to

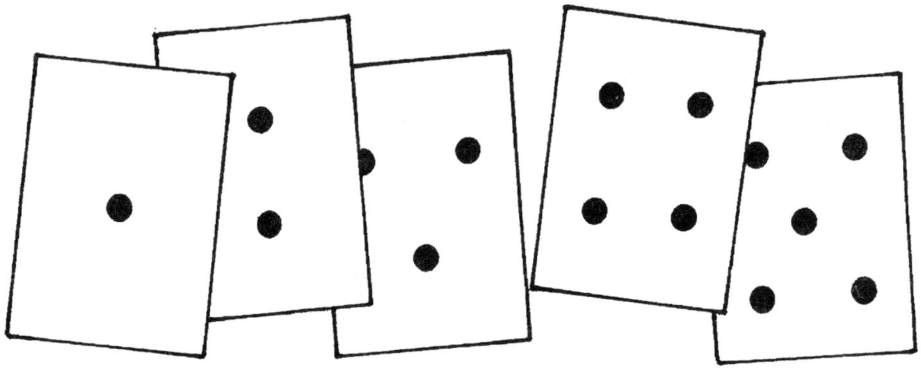

HOME CONNECTION

Announce that you are collecting bottle caps for a classroom game. Set a specific amount of time—for example, one week—and have the children bring in all the bottle caps their families were able to save during that time.

Purpose: In this activity, children learn to associate tangible items with numerical values.

Materials:

10 unlined cards or thick paper (cut to 12 cm. x 18 cm.)
stapler
55 bottle caps
marker

Preparation:

1. Cut 10 cards out of thick paper (or use unlined cards).

2. Mark 1 to 10 dots (not numbers) on the cards.

3. Collect 55 bottle caps.

4. Make an envelope out of thick paper (with stapled sides) to hold the cards and bottle caps.

Activity: Using a set of cards, ask a child to match the number of bottle caps to dots on the cards. Count together the number of bottle caps.

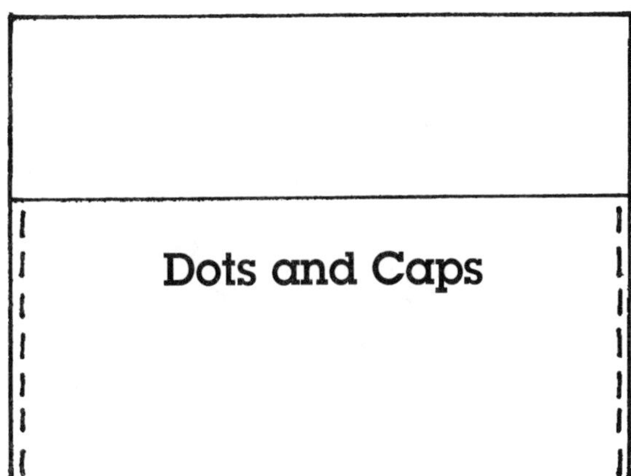

Extensions and variations:

- Show a younger child a card with 1, 2, or 3 dots and ask what number the card represents.

- Ask a child to close his eyes. Hide one of the cards. When the child opens his eyes, can he say which card is missing?

 to 

Number Puzzles

HOME CONNECTION

This activity can be made into a permanent game for the classroom if parents are willing to make the number puzzles on cardboard. In this way, parents can help at home to support classroom activities.

Purpose: The 6 puzzles described in this activity have a variety of uses in the classroom. Number puzzles give children needed opportunities to experience mathematical relationships through the manipulation of concrete objects. By observing the children, the teacher recognizes when a child is ready for the next step, that is, higher number puzzles. The puzzles are designed so that children will associate a specific quantity of dots with the corresponding numerals. As they begin to associate symbols with objects, they learn that amounts are represented by particular numerals.

Materials:

6 unlined cards
scissors
marker
thick paper

Preparation:

1. Using a marker, write the numeral on one half of a card and make the corresponding number of dots on the other half. (Laminate the cards or cover with clear contact paper, if possible.)

2. Cut each card in half, using a different cutting pattern—saw-toothed, straight, curve, etc.—for each card.

Activity: Lay out all of the pieces face up on a table. Let the children match the dot half to the numeral half of the puzzles. Then, one or two children play "find the number." They place all of the dot cards face down in a stack and all of the numeral cards face up on the table. Children take turns selecting a dot card and placing it on the appropriate numeral card. The shape of the card also guides them to identify the correct half. The game continues until all dot cards have been matched to the numeral cards. The teacher encourages children to express their understanding of number and quantity by asking questions such as, "How did you decide to put those pieces together?" "Why did you match them?" "Are you sure?"

Extensions and variations:

- Have the child order the number puzzles from 1 to 6. Are the puzzles ordered from left to right? Are the numbers facing in the right direction?

- A variety of games can be "invented" by the children using the number puzzle cards. Encourage them to make up their own games.

to

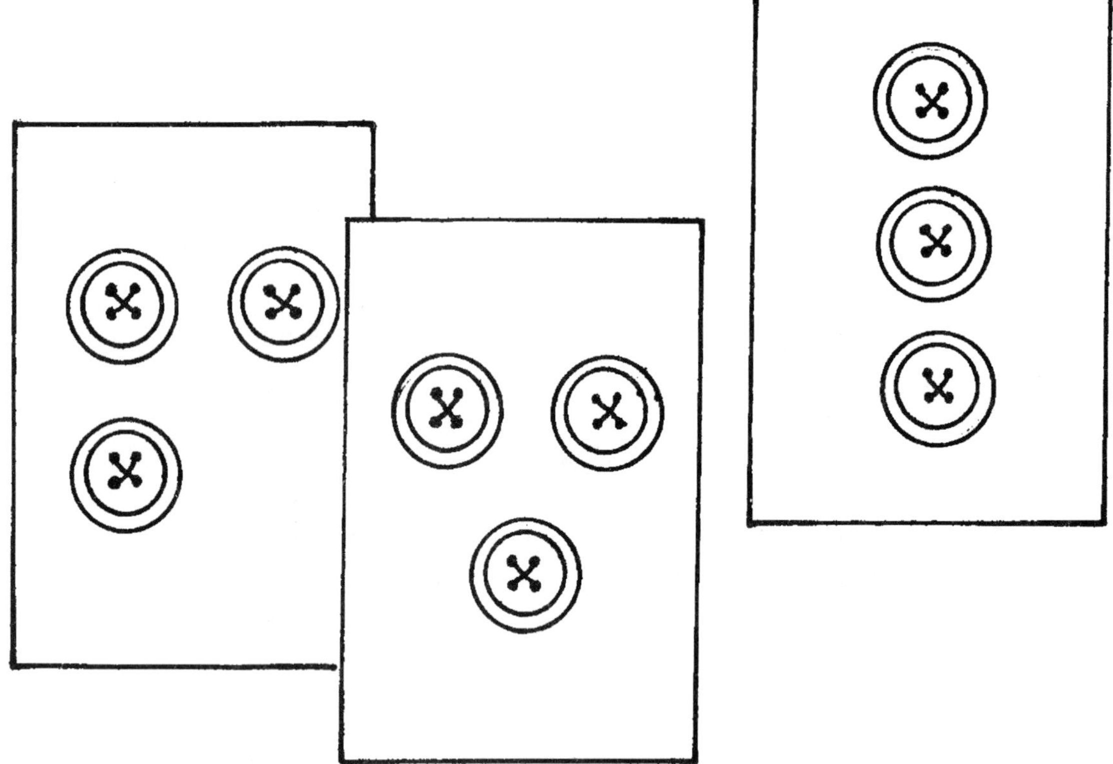

HOME CONNECTION

A simple matching lotto game can be played at home by children and parents using a deck of cards.

Purpose: This activity helps children understand the concept of "conservation of number" (although the arrangement of a set of objects differs, the quantity remains the same). See the illustration showing 3 cards with the same quantity of objects in different locations.

Materials: 8 cm. x 13 cm. cards
markers or dot stickers

Preparation:

1. Make 18 cards, 8 cm. x 13 cm.

2. Place 1 to 6 dots on each card in various arrangements.

3. Have at least 3 different dot arrangements for each number.

Activity: Place all cards on the floor. A child or a pair of children can sort the cards for each number. Some children may be ready for a culminating activity of placing the stacks of cards in order from 1 to 6.

Extensions and variations:

- Make a set of cards from 1 - 6 by sewing the appropriate number of buttons on each card. There should be three different button arrangements for each number.

Number Lotto

 to 

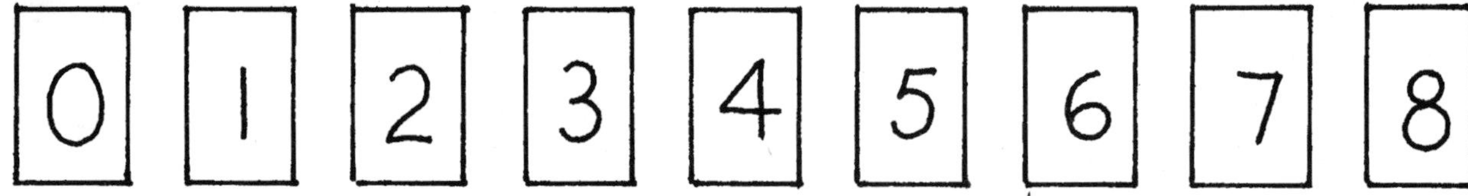

0 1 2 3 4 5 6 7 8

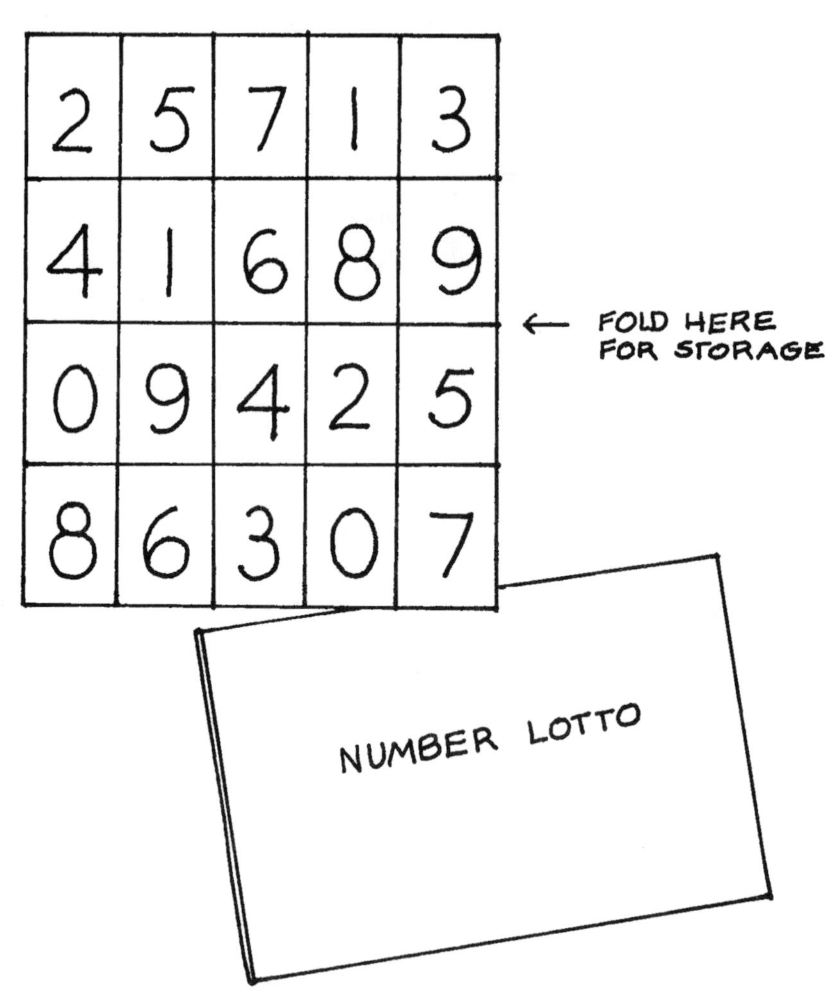

Purpose: Number lotto is a great way for a child to learn to read numerals and associate them with the amounts they represent. After a child demonstrates an understanding of the amounts from 0 to 9, she is ready to work with the number symbols. Playing number games such as lotto helps to integrate number awareness into a child's daily life. Having numbers displayed on birthday, job, and schedule charts and other classroom materials will illustrate that numbers are all around us and essential in daily life.

Materials:

cardboard	ruler
pencil	scissors

Preparation:

1. Make 20 5 cm. x 5 cm. cardboard number cards.

2. Take a 26 cm. x 26 cm. piece of cardboard and section it off so that it can accommodate 5 number cards across and 4 cards down. This is the lotto board. Next write a numeral from 0 - 9 in each of the sections. Write the numerals out of order. Each numeral will appear twice.

3. On the 20 number cards made in Step 1, write the numerals 0 - 9. (One number to a card. Each number will appear on 2 different cards.)

Activity: One or 2 children can play number lotto. Begin by placing the number cards face down in a pile. If 2 children are playing, they can take turns selecting a card and placing it on the appropriate number space. The game continues until all cards have been placed on the number spaces. Teachers can assess whether or not a child can match numbers and name them.

Extensions and variations:

- The lotto cards can be used for a number concentration game. Two or three children can play this game. Cards are spread out face down on the table. Children take turns turning over 2 cards at a time. If the cards match, the child keeps them; otherwise the cards are returned to their original position. The game is over when all cards are picked up.

Number Book

 to 

Purpose: The number book reinforces the concept that numerals represent tangible objects. Children associate the numeral with objects that they can touch and count. This activity shows teachers how to make books. Making one's own book can be a useful and rewarding effort for teachers.

Materials:

- thick colored (or white) paper (30 cm. x 45 cm.)
- heavy paper for two covers (22 cm. x 30 cm.)
- glue
- ruler and pencil
- exacto knife

Preparation:

1. You will be folding a piece of paper (30 cm. x 45 cm.) like a fan to form the spine or back of the book. Begin by folding the sheet of paper in half and with a ruler mark off lines from the center fold at 2 cm. intervals. For a 6-page book, you will need 13 lines.

2. Start to fold on each of the lines. See the illustration for the 6-page book.

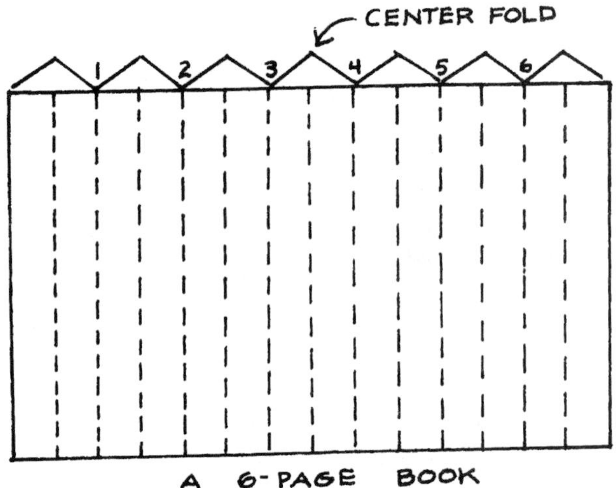

HOME CONNECTION

Invite an older sibling or relative to visit school and make books with the younger children. The children can choose the objects to be glued. They will then have number books that they helped make!

3. After computing the fan folds, stop and do some planning. Decide on the number sequence you want to show, 1 - 5 or 1 - 10, etc. Make some special pages by folding your pages in half and placing a piece of cardboard in between them.

CENTER FOLD

TOP VIEW

1 2 3 4 5 6

Cut out a window. Write the numeral on the paper that shows through the window. Do this for each page to show the number sequence presented in the book.

4. Glue in the double pages. Make sure to glue each long edge of the page right into the fold.

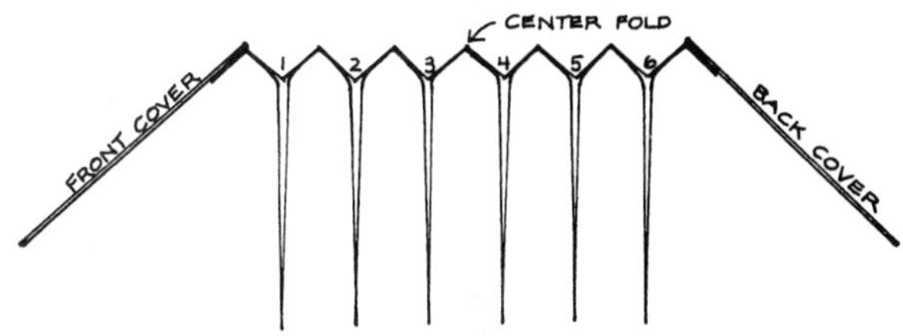

5. Glue front and back covers on the book.

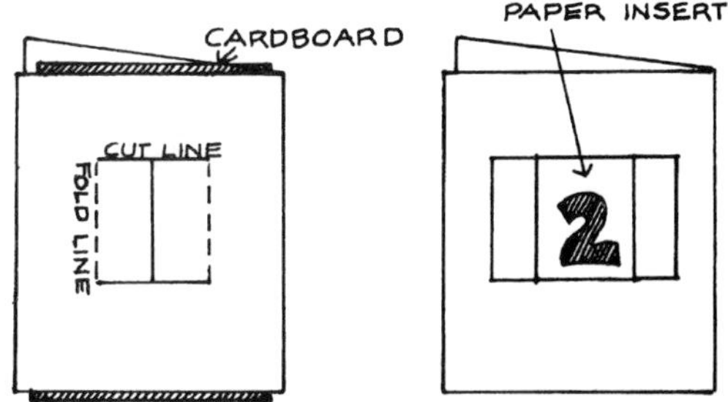

6. Go back to the first window page showing number 1 and glue 1 object, such as a feather, on the page. Do the same for each window page that shows a numeral. Glue corresponding amounts of objects to the page. Use different objects for each page, such as pieces of straw, sticks, paper clips, etc.

Activity: A number book can be used to introduce or reinforce counting and one-to-one correspondence (matching number names to the objects in a set). In small groups or individually, give children repeated opportunities to count the sets of objects on the pages in the book. These counting experiences will help children establish important number concepts beyond rote counting.

Extensions and variations:

- Have children make their own number books. Children can select from among a variety of objects to glue on the pages in their books. The teacher and volunteer parents can help bind the books.

 to 

Butterfly Counter

Submitted by Step by Step Moldova

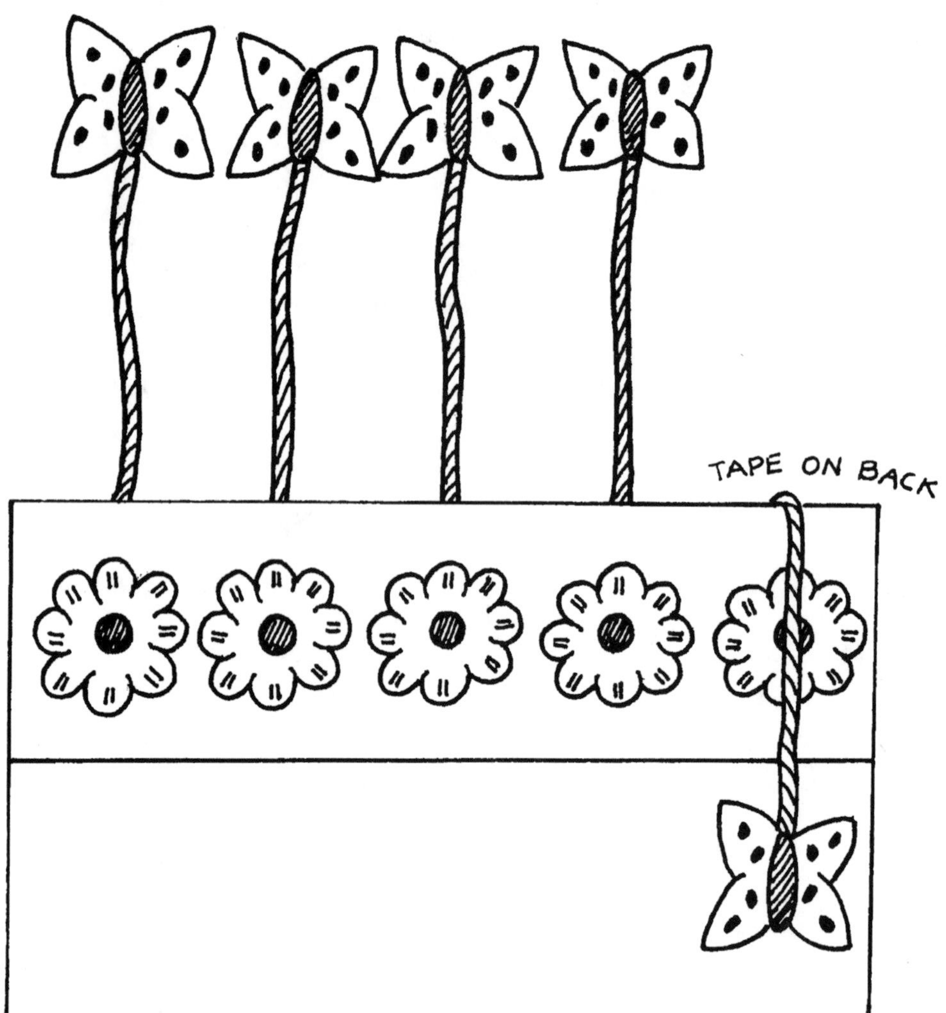

HOME CONNECTION

Let parents know that young children are working on mathematical concepts in their own way from a very early age. Parents should watch for times when their child seems intent on getting just the right amount of something or matching objects accurately. They should play simple counting games such as this one with their child without pressuring the child for speedy computation.

Purpose: Butterfly counter is a mathematical game. It teaches the concepts of one-to-one correspondence and equal/unequal amounts. At this point in their development, young children do not need to know numbers or be able to count. Later, when children understand counting, butterfly counter is a valuable activity that gives practice in addition and subtraction problems from 0 to 10.

Materials:

- paper
- glue and tape
- ruler
- crayons or markers
- string or yarn
- scissors

Preparation:

1. Cut a piece of paper 22 cm. x 15 cm.

2. Hold the paper lengthwise and draw 5 flowers of similar size (approximately 3.5 cm. in diameter) and color. The flowers should be evenly spaced.

3. Draw 5 butterflies of equal size (about 3 cm.). Cut them out. Color both sides of the butterflies and glue or staple them onto a string or piece of yarn (approximately 13 cm. in length).

4. Attach yarn pieces to the back of the card so that they line up with the flowers.

Activity: When presenting this activity to young children, flip the butterflies so they appear to be flying above the flowers. Then say, "Now have each butterfly fly to its flower. Are there as many butterflies as flowers?" This experience encourages the development of one-to-one correspondence.

Butterfly counter is an activity that children can use at different levels of understanding of addition and subtraction. The teacher asks questions to show children how to use this learning tool: "How many butterflies are there? How many flowers are there? Look, one butterfly flew away (the butterfly is flipped behind the flower). How many butterflies are left? What would happen if 2 butterflies flew away?"

Extensions and variations:

- Plant a "butterfly" garden using plants that attract butterflies. Make a sign for the butterfly garden and display it in the garden.

- Write a class story about planting the butterfly garden or take pictures of planting and growing to help children recall and describe the process.

Geoboard

3 to 6

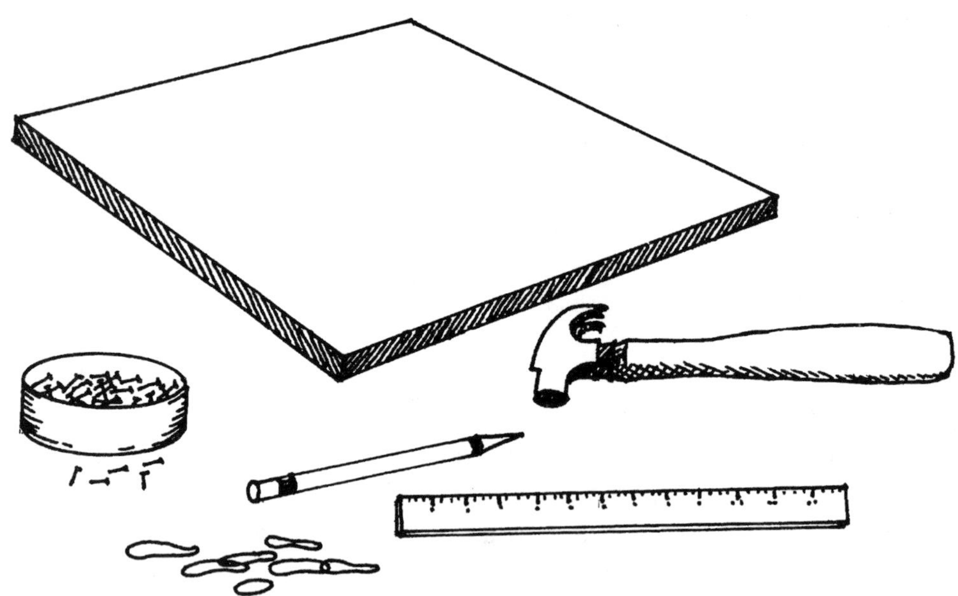

Purpose: The purpose of this activity is to make a classroom object called a geoboard, which is a resource for mathematical learning. Geoboards are square, wooden boards studded with small nails across which rubber bands stretch to form various shapes. Recognizing, forming, and communicating about geometric shapes are important mathematical skills for young children to attain. A multitude of learning activities are provided by the use of a geoboard and rubber bands. As children begin to develop an awareness and appreciation of geometric shapes in their environment, they will become better able to describe and classify them. Geoboards help children begin to understand the relationships among shapes. One distinct advantage of the board is that it can be rotated.

Materials:

- hammer
- pencil
- 25 nails per board
- ruler
- rubber bands (colored if possible)
- wooden boards 1.5 cm. to 2 cm. thick (to make 30 cm. squares)

HOME CONNECTION

Ask parents to saw the wooden pieces for the boards. This is a good way to involve them directly in the classroom by doing the measuring and cutting with a small group of children.

Preparation:

1. Cut 1.5 cm. - 2 cm. thick boards into 30 cm. squares.

2. Each board requires 25 nails, about 2 cm. long. Hammer the nails into the board in a 5 x 5 arrangement.

3. Collect rubber bands in a variety of colors and sizes.

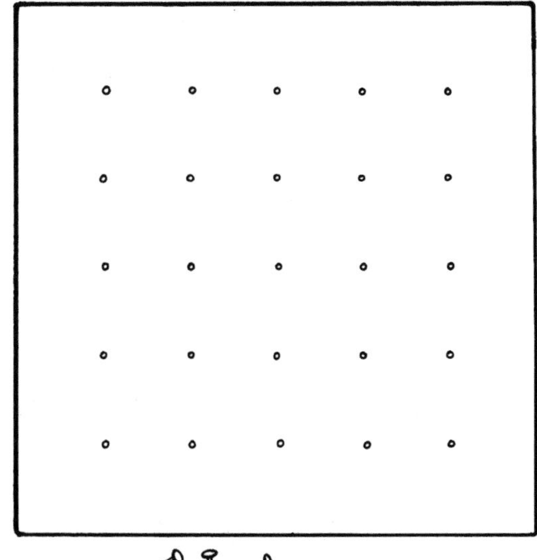

Activity: Encourage children to experiment with the geoboards by stretching rubber bands around the nails. Without models, allow the children to independently create designs and shapes. Encourage them to talk about what they are doing. Children sometimes make up names for what they create. Some children recognize shapes and can name them. When they do, casually ask questions such as, "How many sides does your square have?" "How many corners does your square have?" "Are there more corners or more sides?" "Can you make another one that looks just like it but is bigger or smaller?" "Does your square look the same if you turn the geoboard around?" When children have created unusual designs, rotate the board. Sometimes that leads to the children giving different names to the same design.

Extensions and variations:

- Encourage further experimentation by giving children different amounts of rubber bands.

- Depending on their age and experience, children will react differently to clues such as the following: "With your rubber bands, make a geometric form with 3 sides (4 sides, 5 sides). What shapes did you just make?" "Is it still a triangle if you turn the board around?"

- Create a shape hunt. Have the children search their classroom for shapes in the windows, doors, chairs, blocks, balls, etc.

- Using water and paint brushes on the playground, have children paint geometric shapes.

Shape and Number Envelopes

 to 

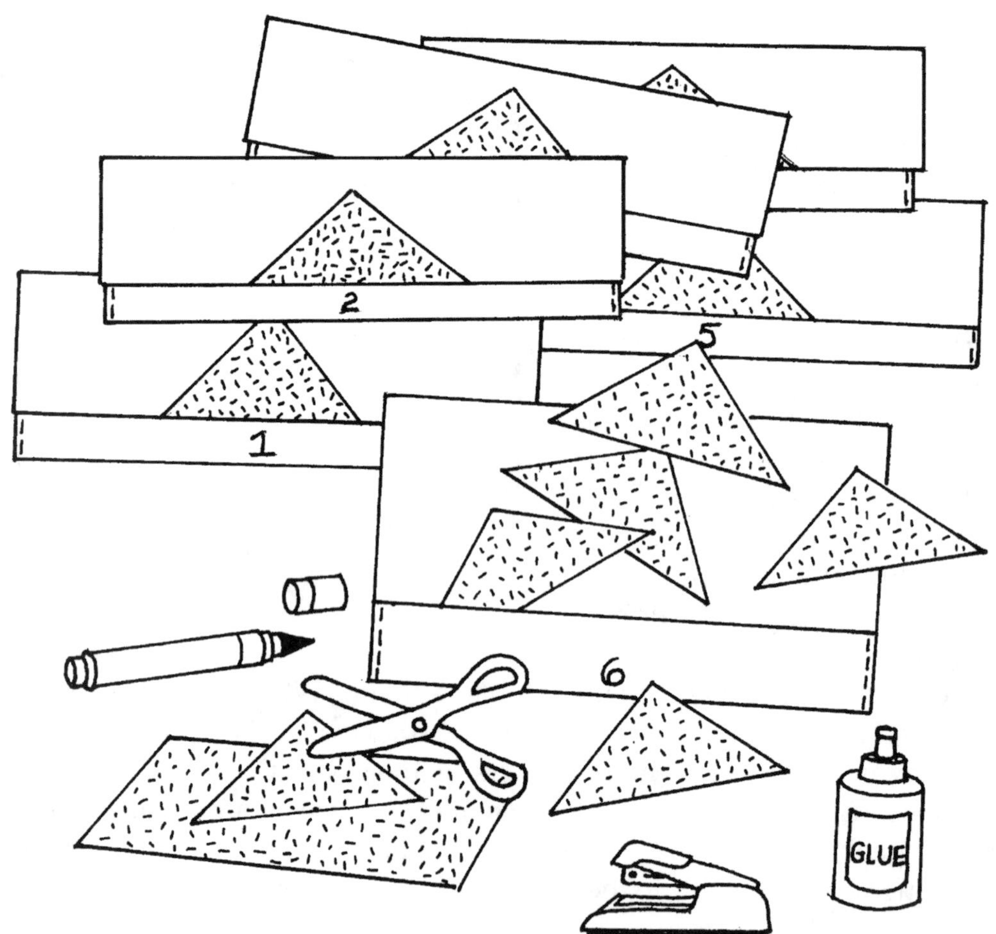

Purpose: Young children need many opportunities to manipulate shapes and numbers for mathematical readiness. This activity combines shape recognition, matching, number recognition, and counting. Children are asked to place the appropriate number of shapes into numbered envelopes. This activity focuses on numbers 1 through 6, but it is easily adaptable to other numbers. When children count and match amounts to the corresponding numeric symbol or numeral, they develop logical reasoning abilities.

HOME CONNECTION

Parents should be informed about the basic concepts being explored with children in class so they can also focus on similar ideas at home. For example, parents can point out various shapes around the house when they know that "shapes" are the focus of a popular game in school.

Materials: glue or stapler
pen and ruler
scissors
thick colored paper

Preparation:

1. Make an envelope by taking a piece of thick colored paper and laying the paper in a horizontal position. Fold the paper 7.5 cm. from the bottom. Then fold the remaining 6 cm. over the bottom portion. Secure the sides with staples or glue. Make 5 more envelopes.

2. Decorate the front of the envelope with a shape, such as a triangle. The shape should be a different color than the envelope.

3. Write a numeral, from 1 to 6, on the flap of the envelope.

4. To fill the 6 envelopes, cut out 21 triangles. Fill each envelope with the number of triangles that corresponds to the numeral written on the envelope. For example, 5 triangles are inserted in the "5" envelope.

Activity: This activity is a good one to use for an individual child. Give the envelopes and shapes to a child. Ask the child to fill each envelope with the number of shapes corresponding to the numeral written on the envelope. Encourage the child to fill all the envelopes. In this way the child begins to associate amount with the representational numeral and begins to practice counting.

Extensions and variations:

- Using the above directions, prepare a set of 6 envelopes with circles, a set of 6 with rectangles, and a set of 6 with squares. Number each set from 1 to 6 and prepare 21 cut-out shapes for each set.

- Place all of the number-shape envelopes in the center of a table. Mix the 21 circles, 21 rectangles, and 21 squares. Invite a small group of children to each take 1 or 2 envelopes, select their shapes, and fill the envelopes with the corresponding shapes. As the children work, ask them to discuss the numerals and shapes they are using.

- Number-shape envelopes can be extended to numbers above 6. Those children who have mastered this activity to 6 can use number envelopes to 10.

 to 

Shape Pair Cards

HOME CONNECTION

Matching objects based on characteristics is a learning game that parents can do at home with their children. Encourage parents to help children find natural pairs of things in the home, such as shoes, socks, mittens.

Purpose: Using shape pair cards is an active-thinking task that encourages children to explore geometric shapes, colors, and the concept of pairs. Young children need changes of pace and time to move around. In this activity, they walk around the room trying to find another child who has a card with the same color and shape. (*"Children can learn as much on their feet as they can on their seat."* —James L. Hymes)

Materials: unlined cards
markers (many different colors)

Preparation:

1. Make pairs of cards with identical colored shapes on them—for example, a pair of cards with yellow circles, a pair with red triangles, a pair with green rectangles, etc. Make the cards approximately 8 cm. x 13 cm.

2. Be sure that there are enough cards for each child to have one.

Activity: Give each child a card. Tell the children that they should find the person who has a card that is exactly the same as theirs. The children then come together in a group and report what shape and color they have, for example, "We have a green triangle."

Extensions and variations:

- The teacher can easily extend this activity by asking the children to observe more details about their geometric shapes—how many sides and corners?

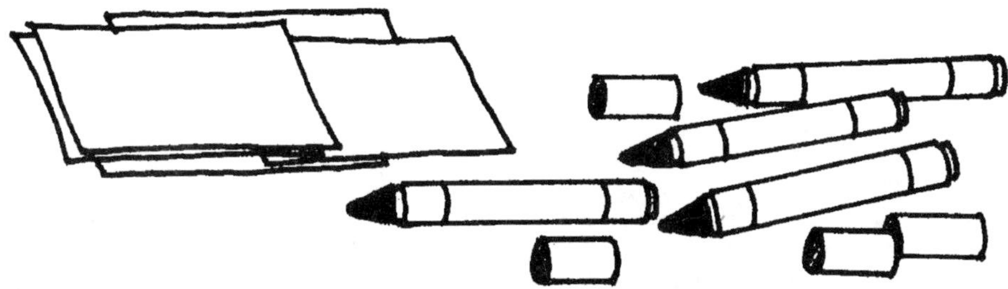

Color Dominoes

 to 

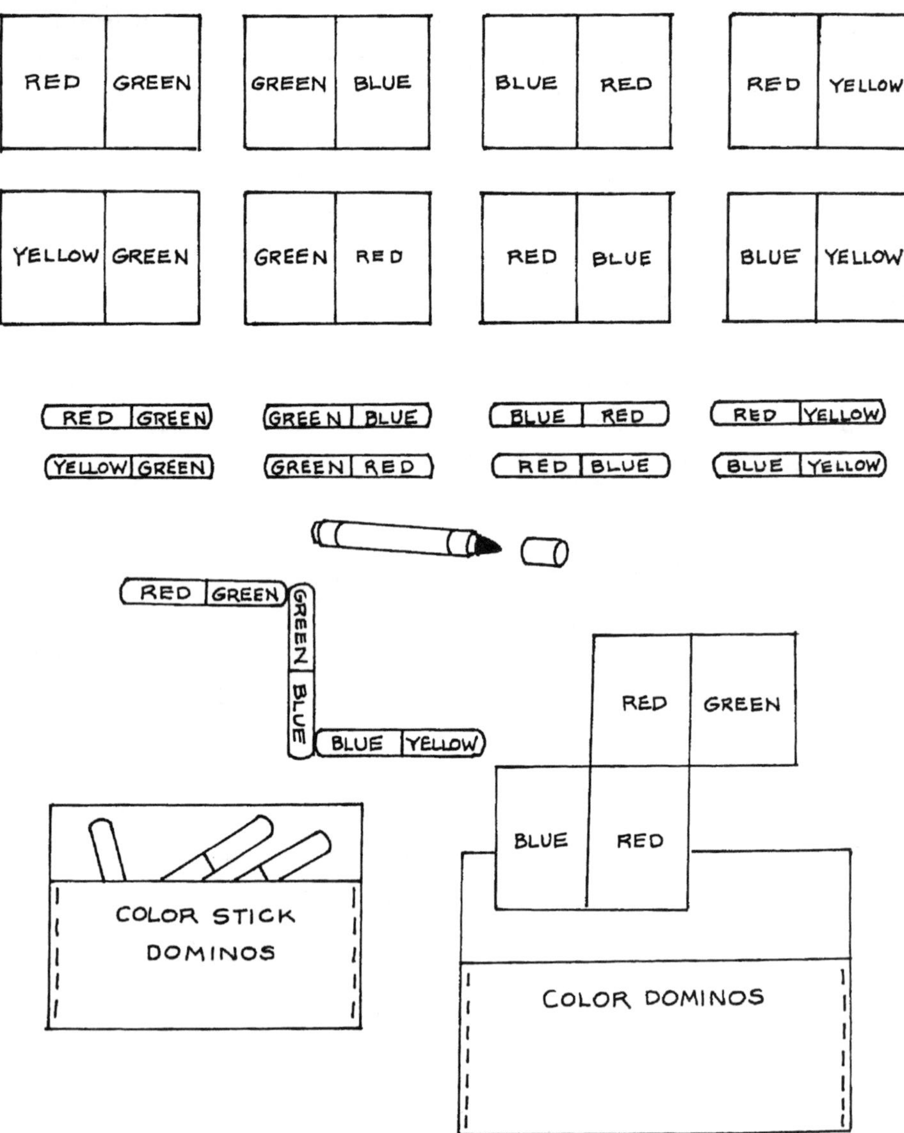

HOME CONNECTION

Children can teach this simple form of dominoes to their parents, grandparents, or siblings. This game is a simple one for children to make at home with parents, too.

Purpose: Using dominoes requires that children observe, compare, identify, and match with one-to-one correspondence. All of these skills are necessary in the study of science and mathematics and in developing early reading skills. Dominoes come in many different forms. This activity suggests several ways that dominoes can meet the age, developmental stage, needs, and interests of children in the classroom. Some sets encourage children to match the number of dots; in others, children match geometric shapes, colors, and leaves.

Materials:

8 unlined cards
black marker
pencil and ruler
thick colored paper
(red, blue, green, yellow)
glue
scissors
stapler

Preparation:

1. Hold each card horizontally and draw a black line from north to south in the middle of the card. The size of the card (the domino) can be approximately 7 cm. x 15 cm.

2. Cut the colored paper into pieces one half the size of the card. Glue one piece of paper on to one half of the card and another piece of paper on to the other half. Use the colors red, blue, green, yellow, as follows:

   Red/Green, Green/Blue, Blue/Red, Red/Yellow, Yellow/Green,
   Green/Red, Red/Blue, Blue/Yellow

Activity: An appropriate game for 3 to 4 year olds is a color dominoes set with each card having 2 colors. Children begin to recognize that there are 2 halves to each domino. The object of the game is to match the color at each end. Have the children work in pairs or alone with the dominoes. Guidance may be given by pointing to each end and asking, "Can you find one with a color like this?" Use the colored paper to make an envelope in which to keep the dominoes.

Extensions and variations:

- A special value of color dominoes is that children can make a variety of sets. Help the children make a set of color dominoes from tongue depressors. Place a black line in the center of the sticks. Give the children one stick at a time and two crayons or markers. Use the pattern listed above.

Shape and Dot Dominoes

 to 

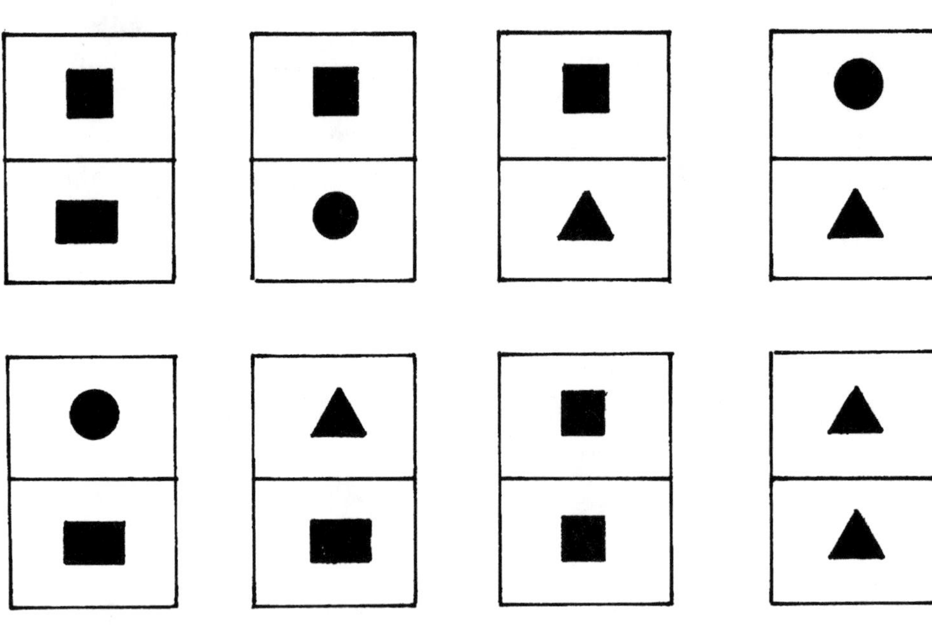

SHAPE DOMINOES

HOME CONNECTION

Invite parents to help supply materials for the classroom by making sets of shape dominoes with their children at home. In this way families know that they are helping their children learn and that they are contributing to the classroom's needs.

Purpose: Repeating an action is important to reinforce learning. Help children to build on their previous experiences with color dominoes by introducing shape dominoes and then dot dominoes. The activities reinforce the concept that there are 2 halves to each domino.

Materials:

- 8 unlined cards
- black marker
- pencil and ruler
- thick colored paper (red, blue, green, yellow)
- glue
- scissors
- stapler

Preparation: Shape Dominoes—Follow directions for making color dominoes on page 37. This time use shapes. Start with squares, rectangles, triangles, and circles. Other sets could include ovals, diamonds, stars, hexagons. Or, try sets with big and small sizes of the simpler shapes.

Preparation: Dot Dominoes—Follow the basic directions for color dominoes. Use small cards.

Activity: Use the shape domino activity first to ensure that children are recognizing that there are 2 halves to each domino. Some young 4 year olds may need help with shape vocabulary.

Use the dot dominoes with the older 4 and 5 year olds. If they need some help, point to one domino and ask if the child can find a domino with more dots, with fewer dots. Using mathematical vocabulary will enhance children's concept development. Make an envelope out of the colored paper to store the dominoes.

Extensions and variations:

- Make nature dominoes. Find pairs of leaves of several varieties. Although no 2 leaves will be exactly the same, children aged 5 or 6 will recognize the similarities. The teacher can comment on how interesting differences are in nature and, of course, in people.

Wooden Dominoes

 to 

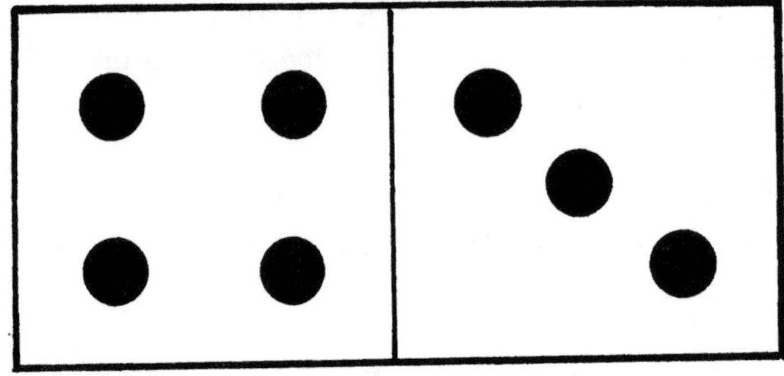

A GOOD SIZE FOR THE WOODEN DOMINO

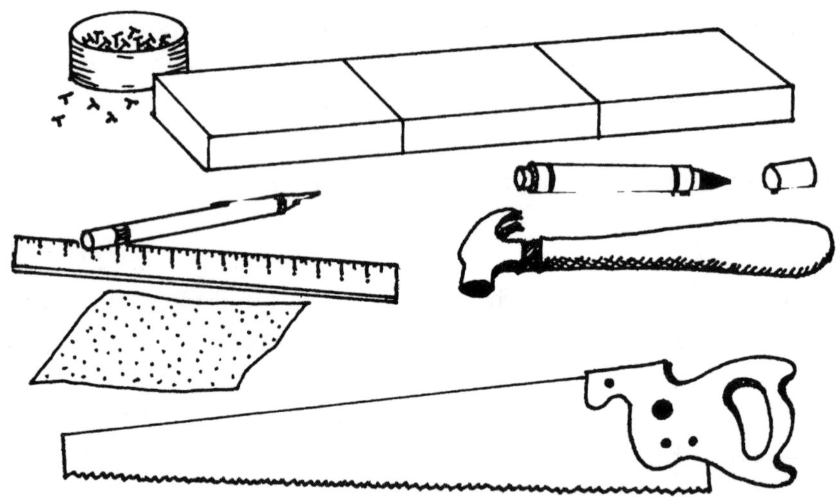

Purpose: This activity reinforces mathematical concepts of measuring and counting as the class makes a complete set of 28 big wooden dominoes. The activity also teaches children how to organize, plan, and work together as a team. It provides physical activity and helps to develop eye-hand coordination.

HOME CONNECTION

This is a great activity for involving families in an activity outside of school. Mothers, fathers, aunts, and uncles can accompany the class on a trip to a lumberyard. If a trip is not possible, some parents may be able to bring wood to the classroom. Woodworking in class is an activity for which extra adults are always needed. Send an invitation home asking for help with the project. Give parents plenty of time to adjust their schedules so that they can participate.

Materials:

- 168 tacks (large heads)
- saw
- marker
- boards of soft wood
- 2 hammers
- sandpaper
- ruler

Preparation:

1. Assemble all the materials. Extra adult help should be available to help manage the woodworking activities.

2. Use a marker to designate the cuts for each domino.

Activity: Take the children to visit a lumberyard. While there, have children handle several weights of wood. Buy enough boards of a soft wood (such as pine) to saw into 28 dominoes.

Back in the classroom, one child at a time should have an opportunity to saw a tile. Other children take turns using sandpaper to smooth the cut tiles. Note the texture of the wood before and after sanding and let the children explore the sawdust.

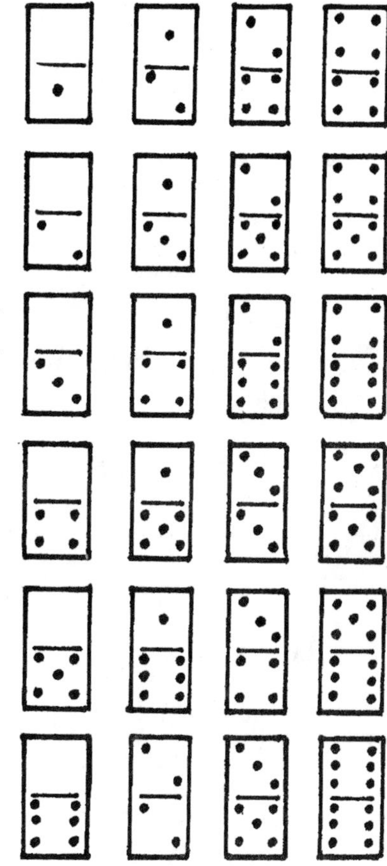

The line between the halves of each tile can either be made with a piece of black tape or a saw. Children with limited or no vision will be able to differentiate sides better if the saw is used.

The children then take turns hammering in tacks to make each dot on the domino. The children will have a sense of accomplishment and will especially enjoy using this set of dominoes. This set (see illustration) includes blanks and doubles tiles, which the teacher must explain.

Extensions and variations:

- With 6 year olds, count the dots on a 6-dot domino. Ask them to select other dominoes that have the same number of dots but in different combinations: 6/0, 4/2, 3/3, 5/1. Demonstrate that the same value is arrived at through different combinations.

The Fishing Pond

 to 

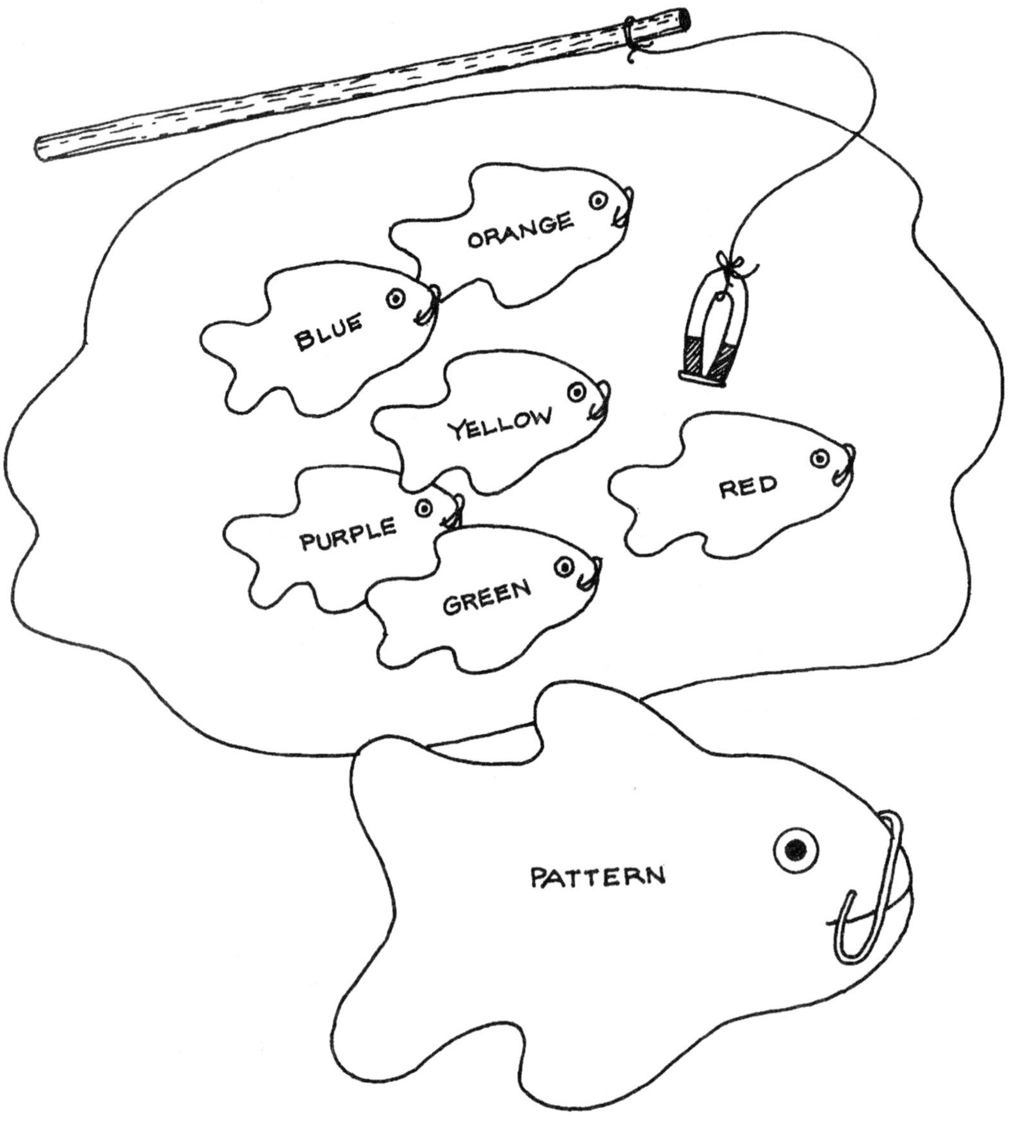

HOME CONNECTION

Ask parents to save wooden dowels or sticks to be used in this activity. Emphasize to parents that learning basic information, such as color names, can be made enjoyable and challenging by using a game format.

Purpose: Learning to group or sort is an important pre-math skill that gives order to a child's world. It is a process, however, that takes time and experience. Because abstract grouping is complex, classification for the young child should be on the basis of easily observed physical properties, such as color, or size, or shape. This activity encourages classifying by color through dramatic play as children use their imaginations to catch colored fish.

Materials:

- thick colored paper: red, blue, yellow, orange, purple, green
- magnet
- blue cloth or cardboard
- scissors
- 6 metal paper clips
- string
- stick or dowel

Preparation:

1. Cut out 6 pairs of fish (12 fish altogether), using different colored paper for each pair. For the youngest children, use primary (red, blue, yellow) and secondary (orange, purple, green) colors. The fish should be approximately 15 cm. long.

2. Attach a paper clip around the "mouth" of one fish in each of the pairs.

3. Make a fishing pole by tying a string around a magnet and attaching it to a stick (or dowel) near one end of the stick.

Activity: Put a blue cloth or piece of cardboard on the floor. Spread the 6 fish with the paper clips on the "water." Tell the children that they are going to go to a pond to catch some fish. Hold up one of the fish without a paper clip and ask the child with the fishing pole to search the pond for a matching fish. When the child catches the matching fish, ask the child what color it is. Repeat the steps by asking another child to fish for a fish of another color.

Extensions and variations:

- By preparing other pair cards, the teacher can extend this game to include vegetables, domestic animals, wild animals, shapes, numbers and corresponding dots, etc.

 to 

Classification by Attribute Cards

Purpose: When children learn about shapes in many different ways, they develop a foundation of knowledge about the properties and relationships of shapes. Classification with the shape cards is an activity in exploring attributes, likeness and differences, and sorting. This activity also helps children to learn to identify 3 shapes, 4 sizes, and 5 colors.

Materials: thick colored paper

Preparation:

1. Make templates out of thick colored paper in triangles, circles, and squares. Cut 4 sizes of each.

2. Cut out each shape in 5 colors.

Activity: Give children sufficient time to look at and play with the shapes during their free-choice periods. In small groups, discuss the various attributes—shape, color, size—and the different ways of sorting them.

In the manipulative center after a child has sorted the cards, say, "Tell me about what you did." Depending on the child's response, you might then ask, "Why does this group of cards belong together? How are the cards alike? How are they different?"

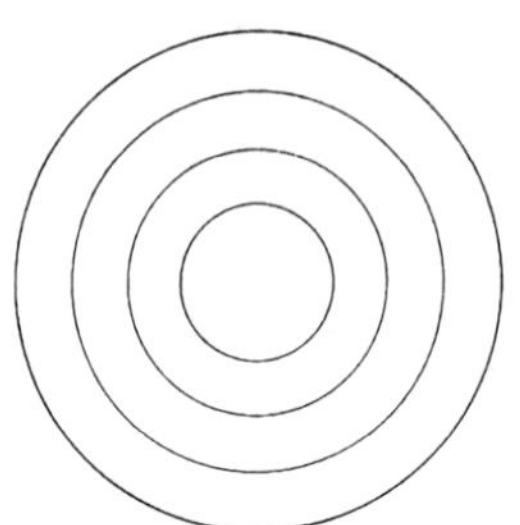

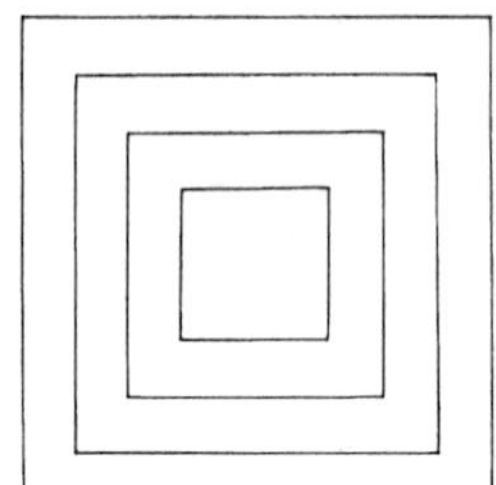

HOME CONNECTION

Playing classification games at home is a wonderful way for children to learn from older siblings and parents and to demonstrate to their family members what they know. A classification game that many children enjoy is to have the people in the game try to guess the animal that one player is thinking of by guessing various possible attributes of the animal.

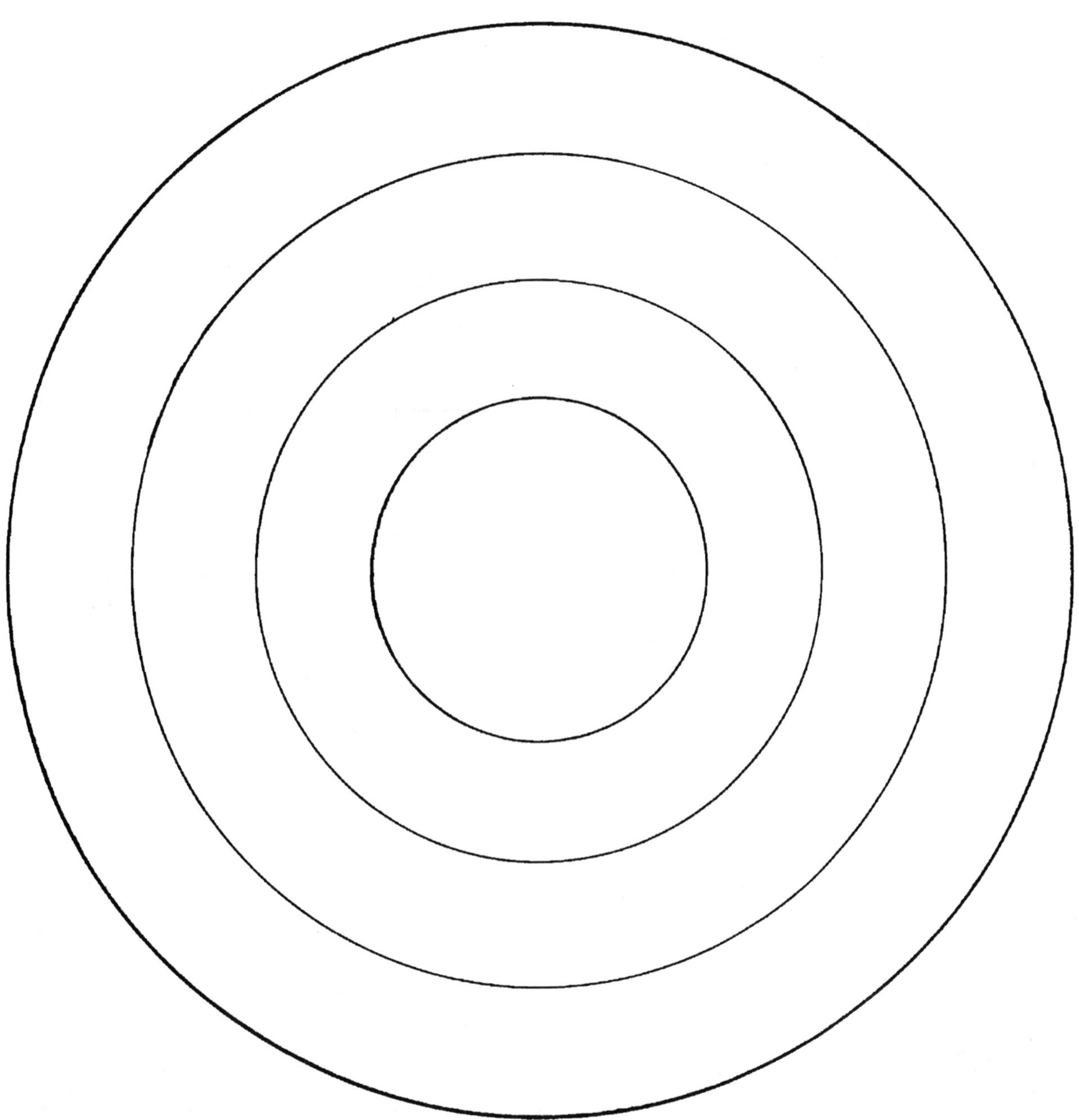

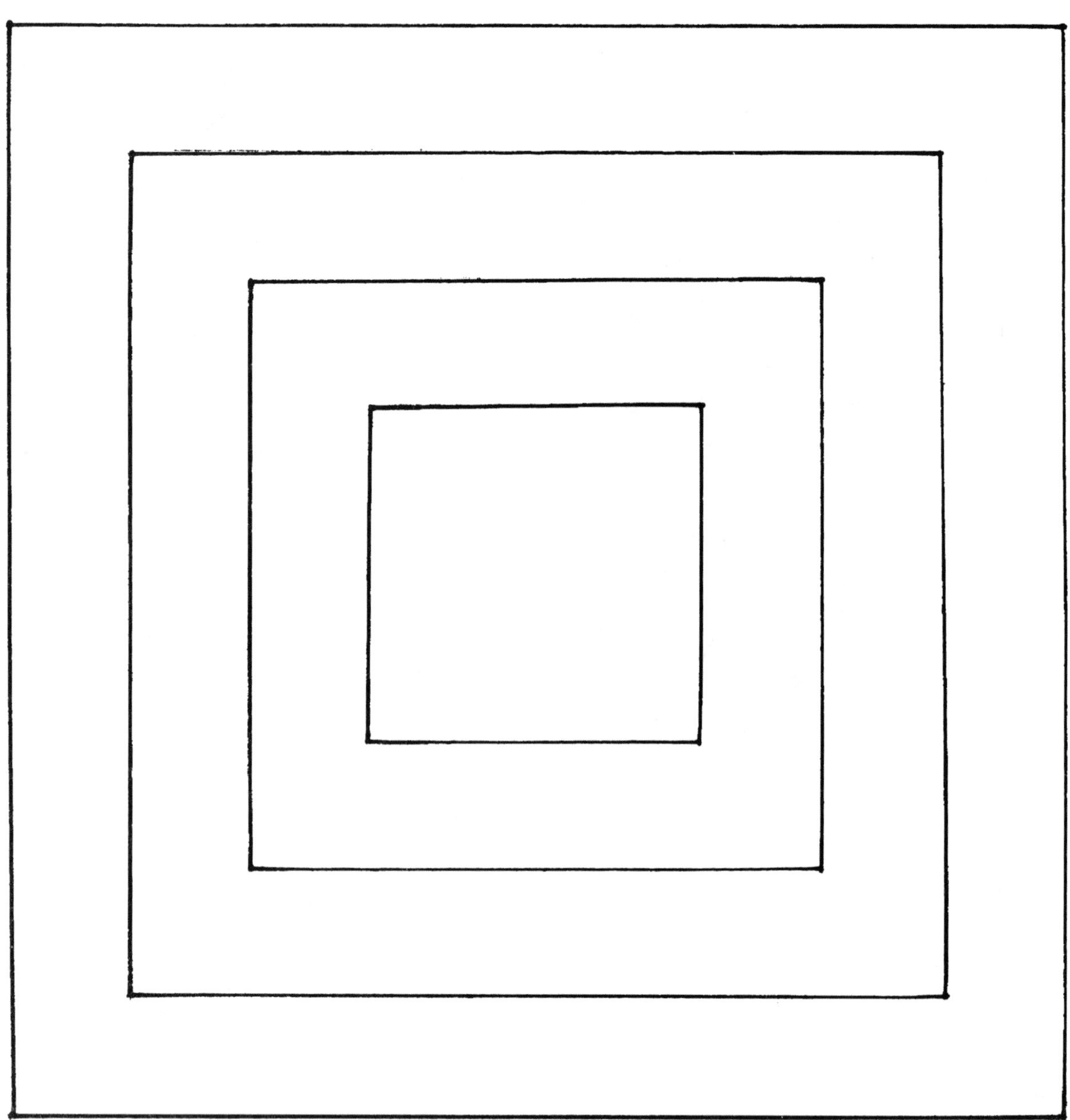

Piaget's Pennies

 to 

Purpose: This is a simple activity to test Piaget's insight that children under age 6, and even some 7 year olds, do not actually understand concepts of numbers. Although they may recite numbers by rote, they do not comprehend the principle that underlies numeration. This activity is designed to encourage teachers and parents to recognize that young children—before they really internalize numbers—need time and opportunity to manipulate, explore, experiment, and make discoveries using tangible materials.

Materials: 10 identically sized chips, coins, discs, or playing cards

Preparation:

1. On a flat, uncluttered surface, arrange 5 chips (or coins, discs, or playing cards) in a horizontal row, but spread them apart. Then, below them, in another horizontal row, arrange the other 5 chips close to one another. See diagram below.

O O O O O

OOOOO

Activity: In a quiet spot with one child at a time, without cues, ask, "Do both of these rows have the same number of chips?" Accept whatever response the child gives. You will find that children of this age will say the top line has more. In the logic of the young child, it if looks like more, it is more. Try moving the chips closer so they match the bottom row. Ask again if the rows have the same number of chips; the child will usually say yes. Separate the chips out and repeat the questions. To use this activity with a large group, glue the chips onto a sheet of cardboard in two rows as described above. This allows more children to see the arrangement because the teacher can hold it up. Do not provide "right" answers. It takes time and experience for children to develop the concept of numerical equivalence.

Extensions and variations:

- Take a ball of clay and make it into a flat pancake. Turn it back into a ball. Ask which has more clay, the ball or the pancake. The children may think that somehow the pancake has more clay because it is wider or conversely that the pancake has less clay because it is so thin. Give a child many chances to work with the clay to experience that the re-formed ball always has the same amount as the pancake.

Geometric Puzzle

 to 

Submitted by Step by Step Latvia and Slovenia

Purpose: The geometric puzzle is a problem-solving activity. Children develop spatial skills when they manipulate the pieces. This kind of puzzle is a valuable mathematical activity because it gives children the experience of looking for a solution in an unfamiliar situation. Children develop their perseverance and patience in seeking solutions. The activity becomes more open-ended by allowing children to create their own geometric puzzles.

Materials: heavy paper
scissors

Preparation:

1. Cut 3 20 cm. x 20 cm. squares out of heavy paper.

2. Draw a 4 x 4 grid on the three squares.

3. Leave one grid blank. On the other two grids, draw the geometric design using markers to color in the squares.

4. Cut one of the grids with the geometric design into small squares. There should be 16 square puzzle pieces.

5. Store the geometric puzzle in an envelope.

Activity: The geometric puzzle is designed to be used by one child at a time. Allow the child enough time to experiment with the puzzle pieces and to create designs on his own. Because problem-solving involves trial and error, let the child try the pieces in a variety of positions. Encourage the child to place the small square puzzle pieces on top of the larger square design. If there is frustration associated with completing the puzzle, talk to the child about the many ways of manipulating the small puzzle pieces to match the identical squares in the grid. Point out that it takes time to solve puzzles and that there is no need to rush.

Those children who easily assemble the geometric puzzle by placing the small pieces on top of the larger square design may want to try a new challenge. Next to the larger square design, place the blank grid. Ask the child to replicate the design on the blank grid. This requires children to use their visual discrimination skills to examine the larger square design and to assemble the smaller puzzle pieces based on what they see.

Extensions and variations:

- Make an open-ended grid by outlining the 20 cm. x 20 cm. perimeter and the 4 x 4 squares. Let the children create their own puzzles by manipulating the shapes into designs. Teachers can copy these and place them in the manipulative area or decoratively hang them around the room.

- In Slovenia, teachers laminate large paintings made by the children and cut them into simple 5-piece puzzles.

- Using attribute cards or wooden blocks, have individual children create designs for others to copy.

- Make simple designs on a geoboard (see page 30). Ask a child or small group of children to copy your design on their own geoboards. Working with simple shapes will help young children build their spatial sense.

 to 

Fruit Graph

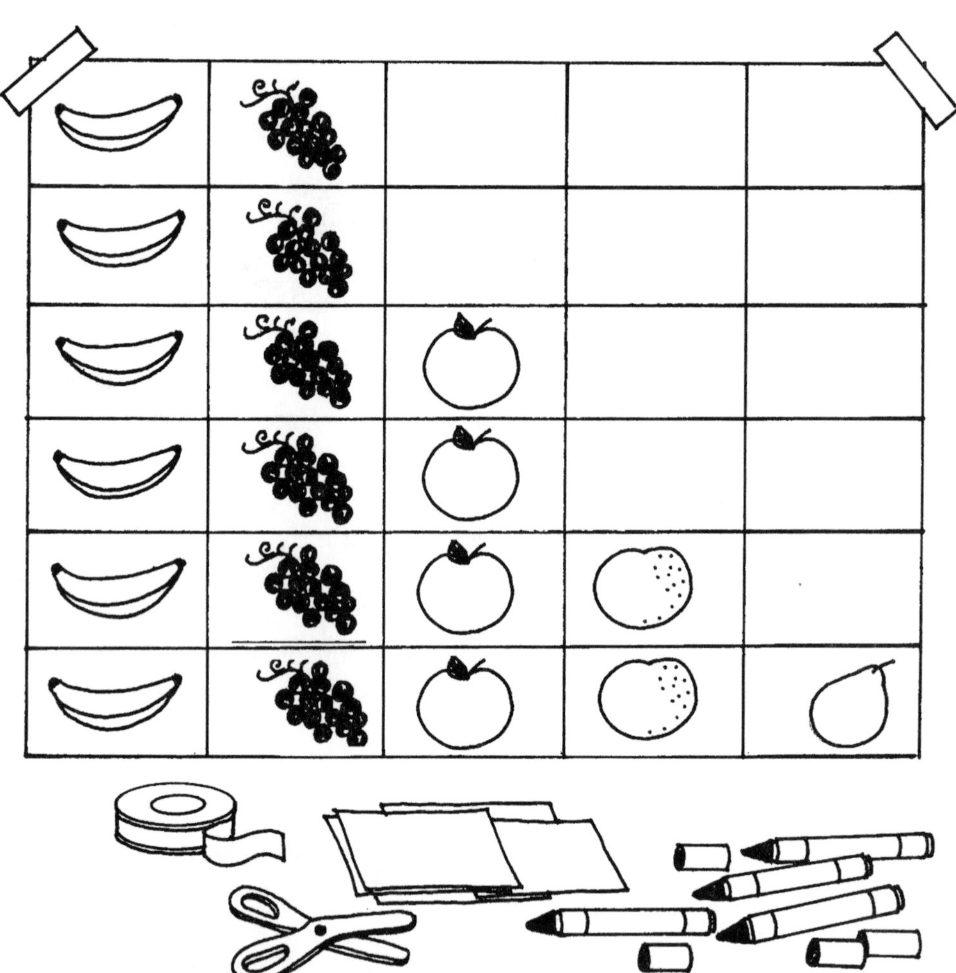

Purpose: Graphing is a great way to organize, display, and compare information. Using pictures, lines, or bars, a graph shows the relationships among choices. Interpreting graphs requires many skills: communication, classification, one-to-one correspondence, symbolization, and measurement.

HOME CONNECTION

Children learn to develop opinions through self-knowledge. Parents who thoughtfully ask their children's preferences and opinions about daily topics are encouraging healthy development. Inform parents when you start this activity, which can extend over a week or so. Ask the children to do some data gathering at home by collecting the names of the favorite fruits of their family members. Include this information on the graph also.

Materials:

small pieces of paper (same color)
scissors
large sheet of paper
glue
old magazines
tape

Preparation:

1. Either draw pictures of fruit or cut out pictures from old magazines.

2. Give each child a small piece of paper (one that is large enough, however, to hold a picture of a fruit that you have drawn or cut out.)

3. Begin this activity at snack time by offering a variety of fruits to the children. Talk about their favorite fruits.

Activity: Ask children to select a picture of their favorite fruits and glue it on the paper.

Sort the pictures by types of fruit. Count the number of papers for each type of fruit. Which fruit has the most? The least? Arrange the fruits in order, from those with the most number of papers to those with the least. Tape the pictures onto a large piece of paper and tape that paper to the wall, making a graphic illustration of the children's favorite fruit.

Ask the children for help in interpreting the graph. Which fruit is the class's favorite? Which is the class's least favorite?

Extensions and variations:

- Other subjects for graphs are birthdays, number of family members, number of girls and boys in the class, type of weather in the month.

- Older children may come up with their own graphing ideas. Encourage children to brainstorm possible topics for graphing.

Birthday Chart	
JANUARY	6 Peter
FEBRUARY	
MARCH	
APRIL	
MAY	
JUNE	
JULY	
AUGUST	
SEPTEMBER	
OCTOBER	
NOVEMBER	
DECEMBER	

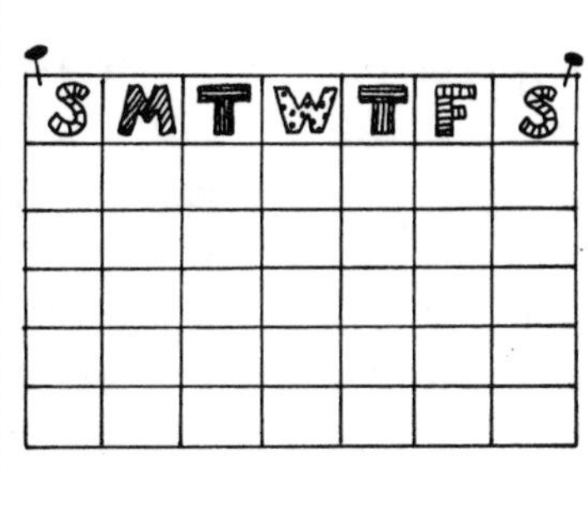

NAME	MEMBERS OF FAMILY
Nick	🯅🯅🯅🯅
Suzana	🯅🯅🯅

 to 

Survey Graph

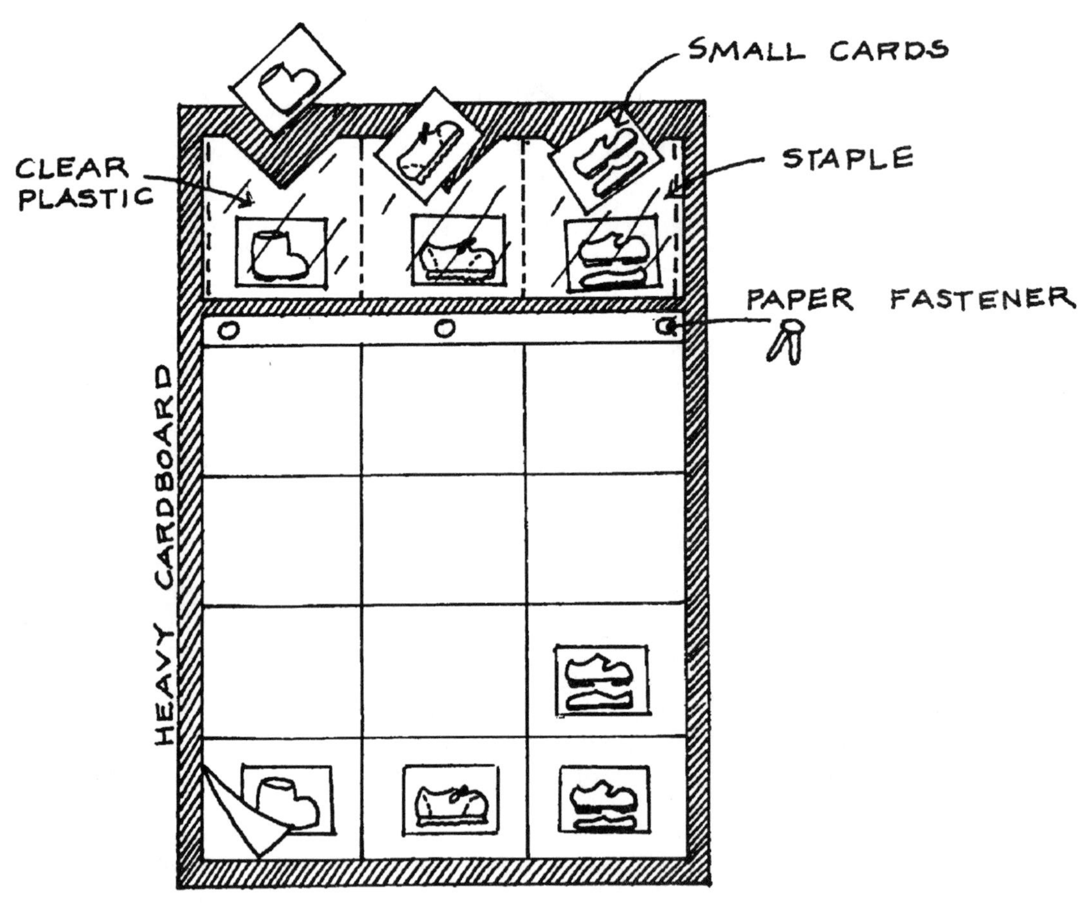

HOME CONNECTION

Children will come to appreciate the importance of mathematics in their daily lives if parents help to point out the various ways information is presented using graphs and charts. For example, parents can show their children newspaper and magazine illustrations that depict graphs, charts, and surveys results. They can set up a simple chart to record daily activities or family preferences. It is best not to use drills or arithmetic worksheets with young children. These are overwhelming for children and often make them dislike mathematics. These drill activities contradict the natural way young children learn mathematics.

Purpose: This simple piece of equipment is a prop to encourage children to conduct surveys whose results are then graphed. It is a device children use to collect and record information from their classmates. Early experiences with comparing, classifying, and communicating develop skills that are important for mathematics and science.

Materials:

22 cm. x 28 cm. cardboard	stapler
marker or colored tape	paper
ruler	tape
heavy clear plastic	brads or fasteners

Preparation:

1. Use a piece of cardboard about 22 cm. x 28 cm. Draw 3 vertical columns each about 6 cm. wide with a wide marker or colored tape.
2. Cut a piece of heavy clear plastic and staple to make 3 pockets. Cut a V-shaped hole in each pocket.
3. Divide 3 or 4 sheets of plain paper about 20 cm. long into 3 vertical columns and 4 rows.
4. Use 3 fasteners to hold the paper to the cardboard (making a "clipboard"). Cover the other sides of the fastener with tape so the children will not be scratched.
5. Draw 3 little pictures and slip one in each of the plastic slots to show the choices in this survey (e.g., boots, sneakers, and shoes).
6. Make 5 - 8 copies of each of the 3 pictures so that the children can pick the picture that matches with what they are wearing.

Activity: Invite 2 children to work as a team to collect and record information about what children in the class are wearing on their feet. Carrying the clipboard and pictures, the polltakers feel very important. As they walk around during activity center time, they are to ask 5 - 8 children, "Are you wearing sneakers, boots, or shoes today?" Then encourage each child to select an appropriate picture. While the interviewed child watches, the interviewer tapes the picture on the clipboard in the appropriate column. A group of 5 - 8 children works well because the group is small enough to complete a graph quickly, yet it is big enough to make the graph show differences in quantities. When the survey is concluded, the top sheet can be put on a bulletin board. In other surveys, children can pick the picture that shows their answer and tape it by themselves onto the sheet.

Extensions and variations:

- Create a Graph Corner. On each graph, write the heading, the children's names, and the date of the graph. Place the graph at the children's eye level. When new graphs are put up, place the old ones in the Family Room.

- Other topic suggestions: favorite juice, color, activity center or book.

Beginners' Tangrams

 to 

Purpose: Tangrams are an age-old game from China. The traditional game is composed of 7 pieces (2 large triangles, 1 middle-sized triangle, 2 small triangles, 1 square, and 1 rhomboid). The traditional tangram is too difficult for young children (and indeed for many adults!) Since playing tangrams encourages an understanding of spatial relationships, however, it is worthwhile to adapt the game for smaller children. This activity is an adaptation for 3 and 4 year olds. It includes 3 large shapes (a square, a triangle, and a rectangle) and puzzles to use with the shapes. Attached are templates of the 3-piece tangram set and 4 puzzles.

Materials:
- scissors
- pencil
- ruler
- black marker
- thick colored paper
- white paper
- templates for square, triangle, rectangle

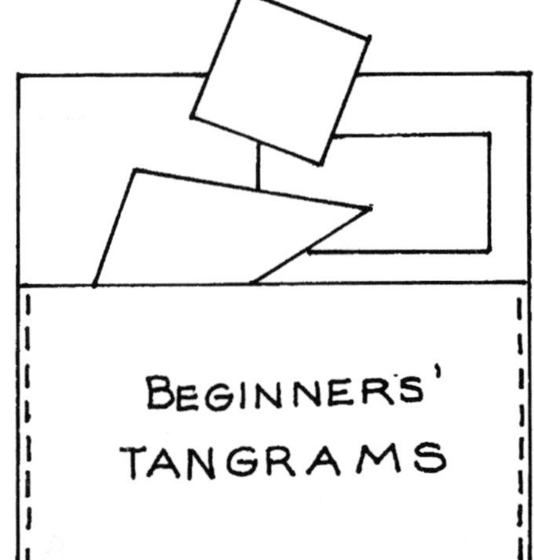

Preparation:
1. Cut beginners' tangrams from thick colored paper, using the attached templates. The tangram pieces can be laminated or covered with clear contact paper, if available.
2. Keep each set of beginners' tangram pieces in a separate envelope.
3. Copy the puzzles onto white paper. Outline the puzzles boldly with a black marker.

Activity: Exploring the shape, size, and the spatial relationships among these 3 pieces is a rewarding activity. Children will enjoy handling the tangram pieces. The first step in establishing geometric concepts is to give them the shapes and let them freely explore them. Using tangrams is an individual task, but you can set up a small group activity by letting 3 children work on tangram puzzles. Each child receives a puzzle and manipulates the tangram shapes to fit it. The puzzles are intended for 2 pieces; others can be 3-piece puzzles. In addition to getting children to think and problem solve, tangrams are good for further developing visual perception and fine motor skills.

HOME CONNECTION

Inform families about the tangram activities before you introduce them to the children. Request volunteers to help cut out the shapes. It would be ideal to have a set for each child. Volunteers from families can help make this happen!

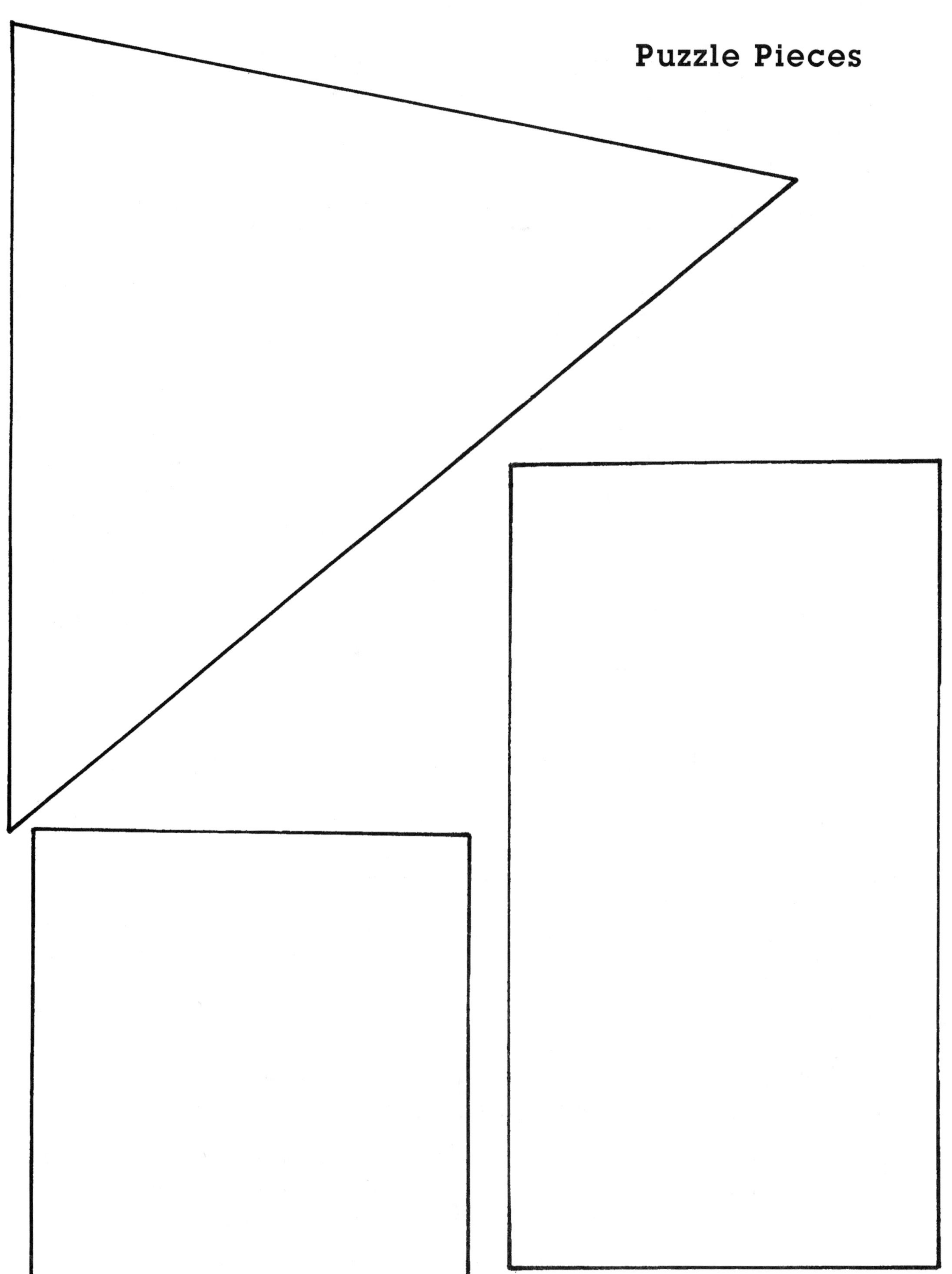
Puzzle Pieces

Beginners' Tangram Puzzle

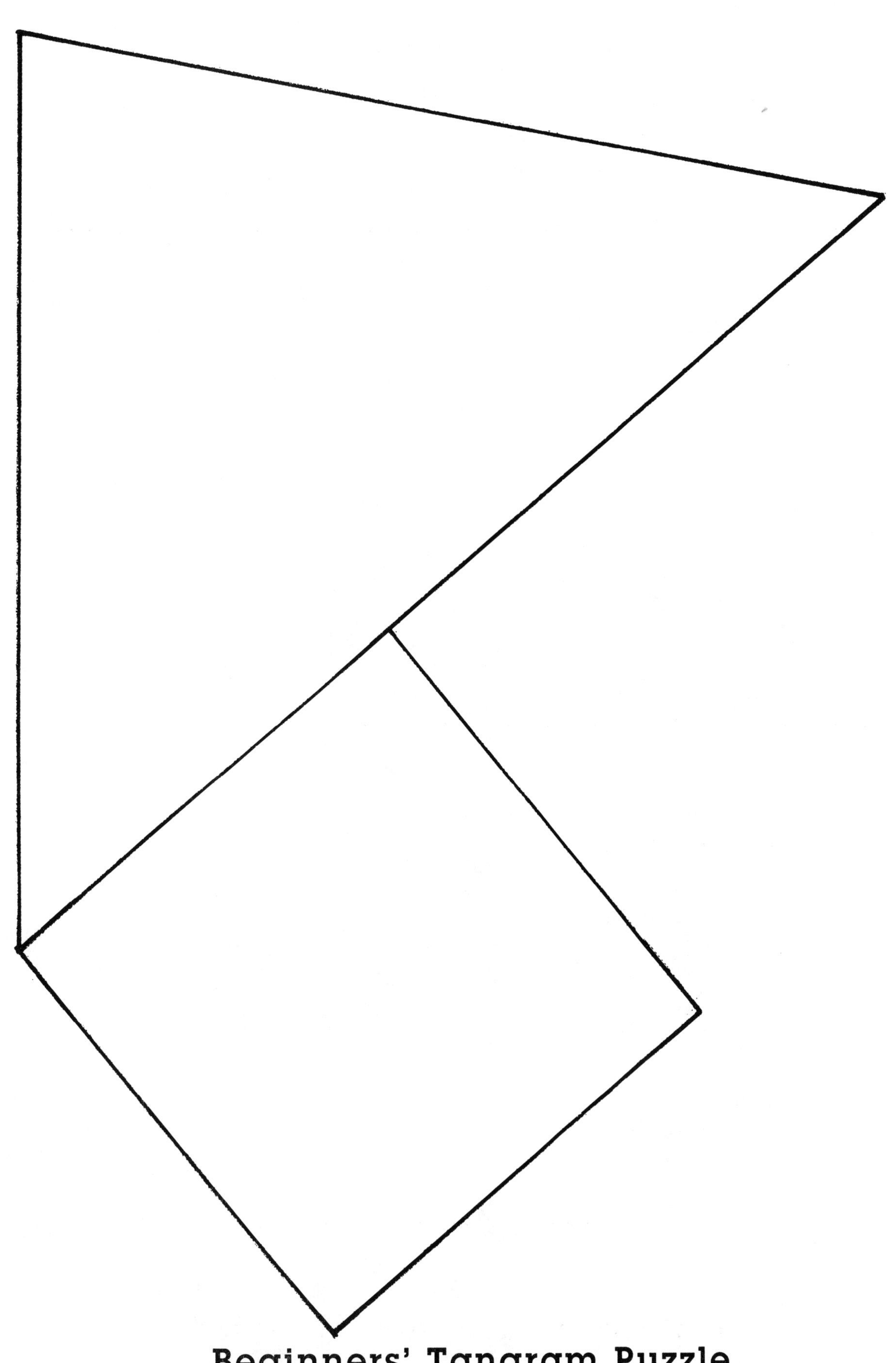

Beginners' Tangram Puzzle

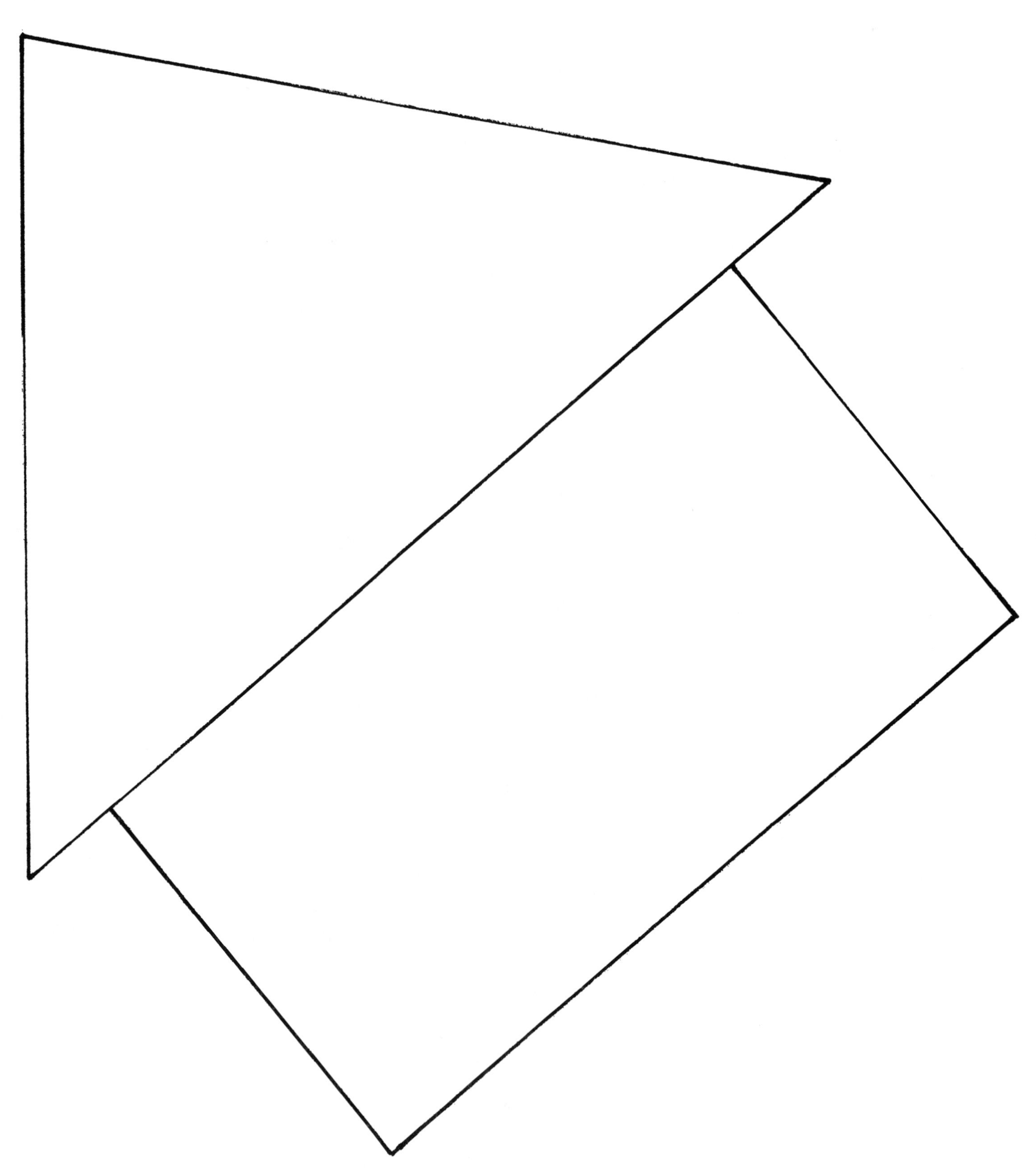

Beginners' Tangram Puzzle

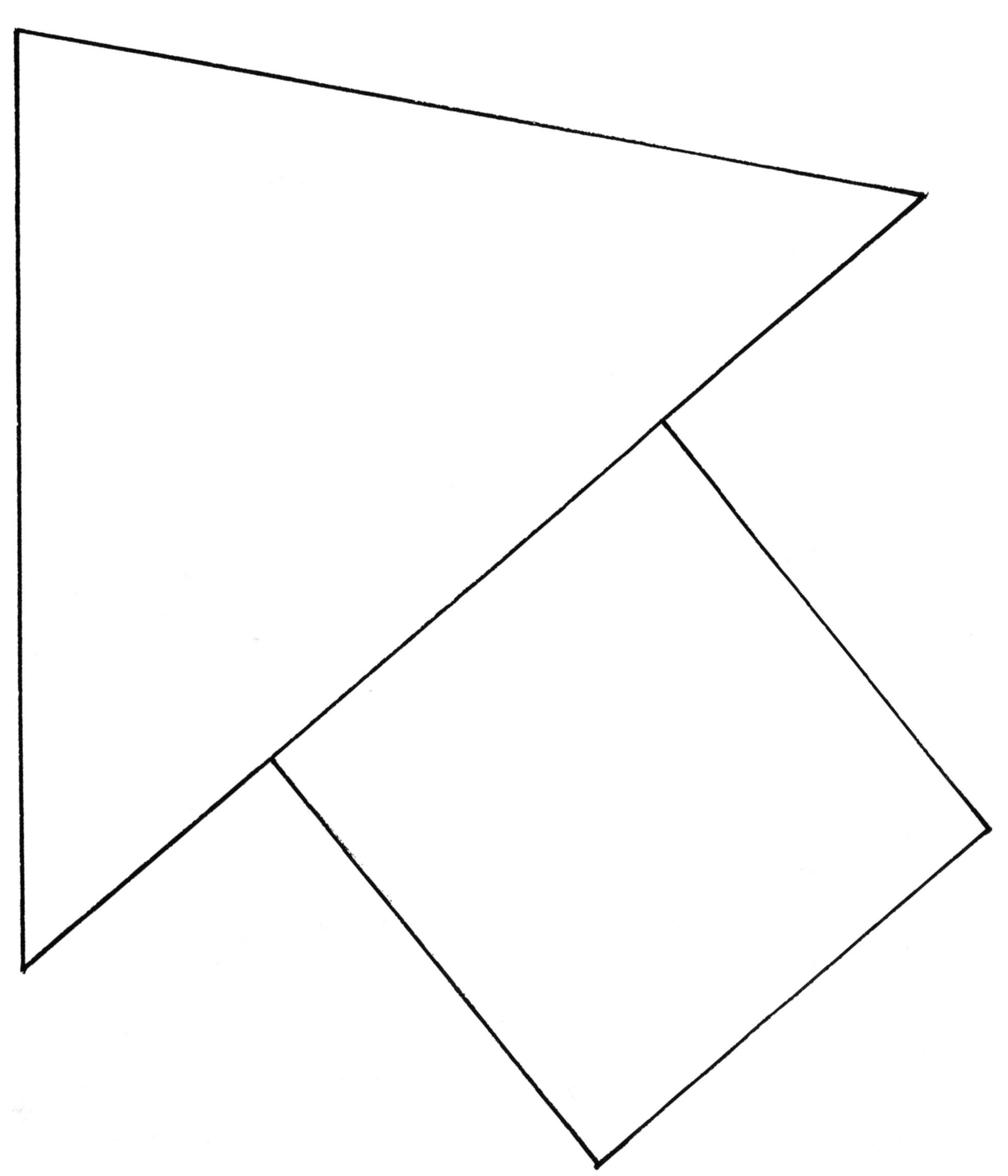

Beginners' Tangram Puzzle

 to 

Intermediate Tangrams

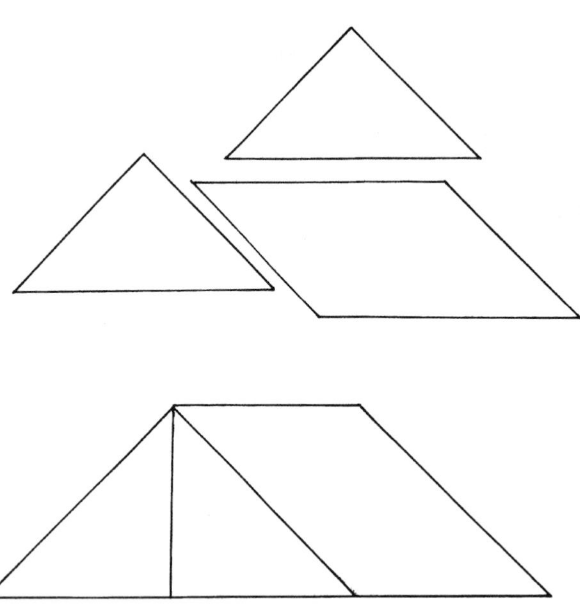

Purpose: In early childhood programs, teachers provide children with varied experiences in geometry. These experiences begin with exploration of familiar objects (blocks and cans) and continue with other shapes to manipulate, such as beginners' tangrams. With the use of tangrams, children will be begin to develop concepts of size, shape, and symmetry. Tangrams aid in developing an understanding of geometric properties and relations. This activity adapts the classical tangram set. Here we use 3 pieces.

Materials:

- scissors
- white paper
- black marker
- thick colored paper

Preparation:

1. Intermediate tangrams include 2 small-sized triangles and 1 rhomboid.
2. Keep each set of intermediate tangram pieces in a separate envelope.
3. Using the attached templates, make the shapes out of thick colored paper. They can be laminated or covered with contact paper. Duplicate the puzzles on white paper and outline boldly with black marker.

Activity: The objective for the children is to explore and experience the many possibilities involved in this spatial relationship activity. Learning the names of the shapes is incidental but will happen by using tangrams. Children can work either alone or in groups of 3. They manipulate the 3 pieces to fit the outlined puzzles. Encourage the children to play with the tangrams and make new patterns.

Extensions and variations:

- Invite the children to make their own puzzles. As they discover new puzzle shapes, help them outline the shapes on white paper. Make the new puzzles available to all the children.

Puzzle Pieces

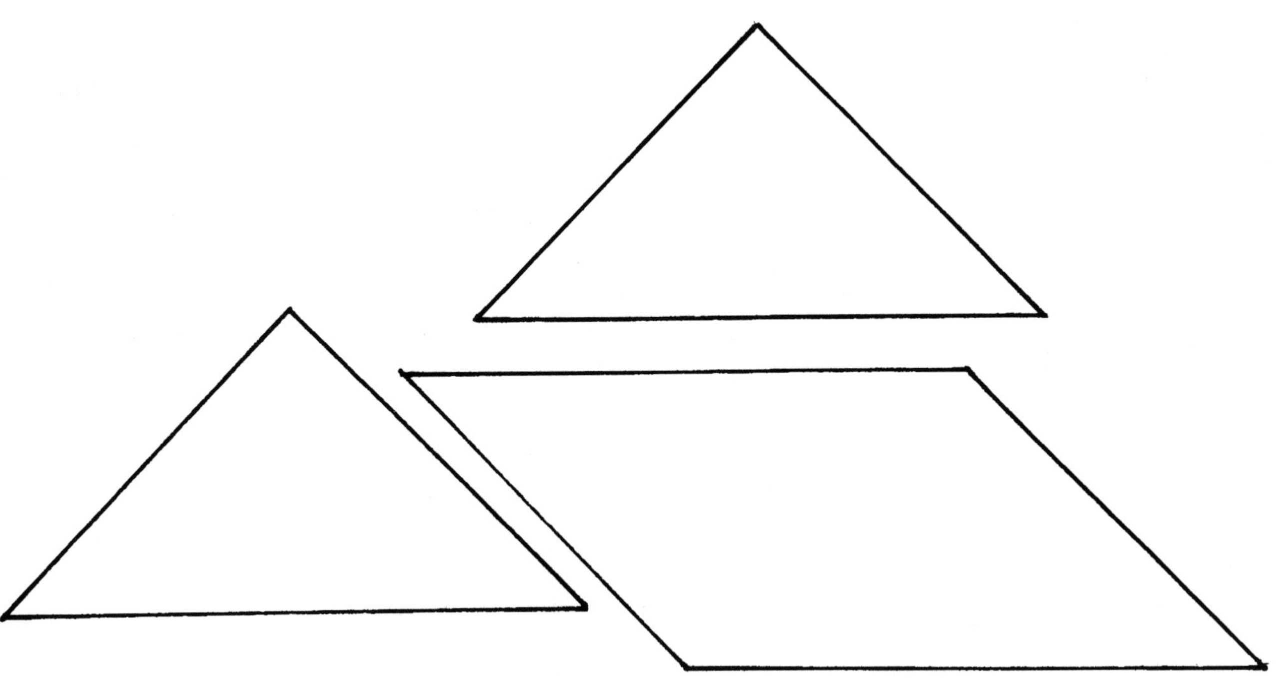

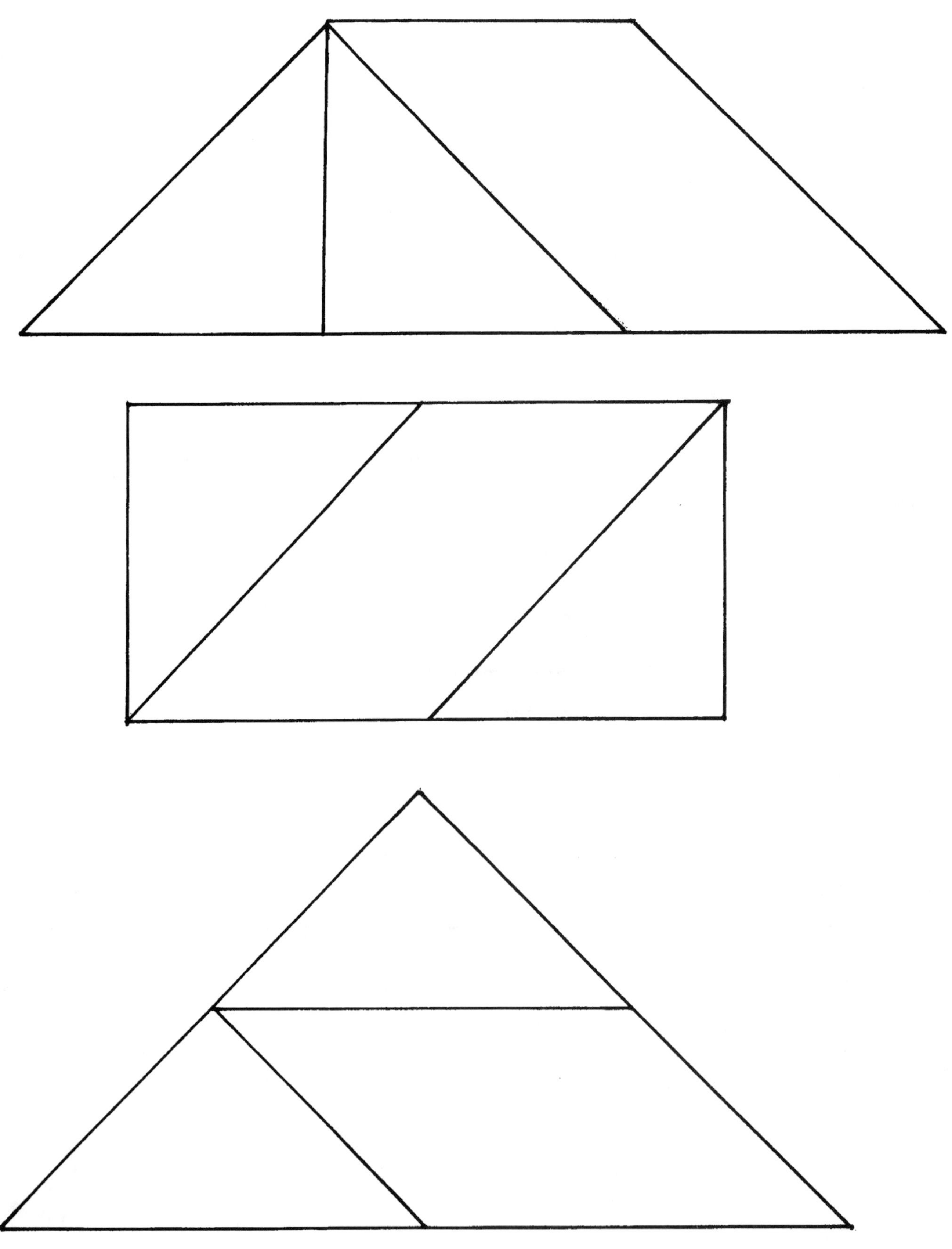

Intermediate Tangram Puzzles

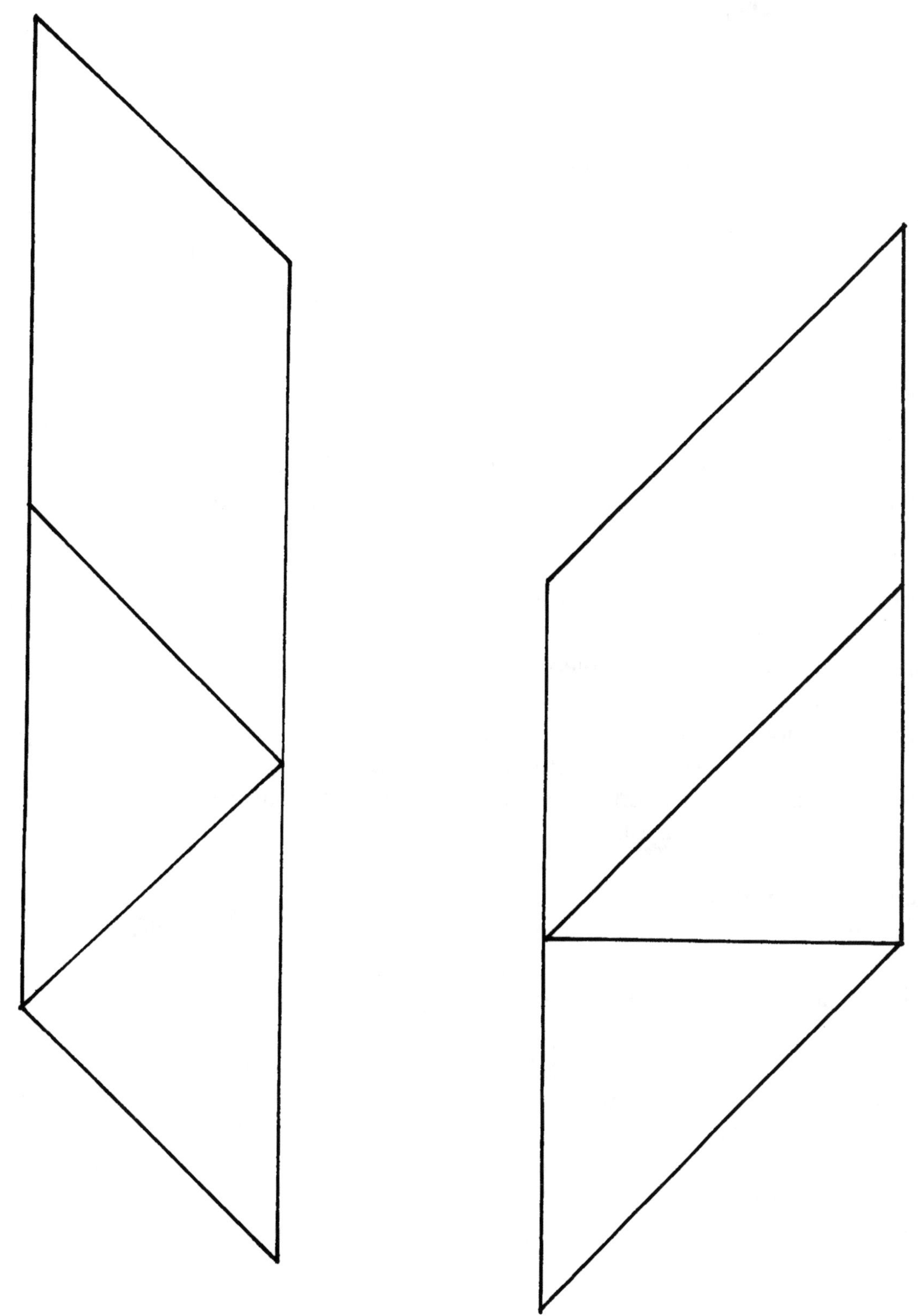

Intermediate Tangram Puzzles

Advanced Tangrams

Purpose: Building on previous experience, some children may be ready to use all 7 tangram pieces to either explore shapes they previously formed (a square, a right-angled triangle, a rectangle, etc.) or make new designs of their own.

Materials:	scissors	white paper
	black marker	thick colored paper

Preparation:

1. Cut out the 7 pieces (2 large triangles, 1 middle-sized triangle, 2 small triangles, 1 square, and 1 rhomboid). Use the attached templates. Laminate the pieces or cover with contact paper.

2. Duplicate the attached puzzles for each child.

3. Store the 7 advanced tangram pieces in an envelope.

Activity: To demonstrate rearranging different combinations to make familiar shapes, ask the children to use all 7 pieces to complete puzzles 1 and 2. If the children become frustrated or bored with these, they may need more time to explore combinations of intermediate tangrams. Answers for puzzles 1 and 2 follow.

Extensions and variations:

- After free-exploration, ask children to use 3 of the smallest triangles to make a square. Children will use their problem-solving skills to manipulate the puzzle pieces into shapes. With practice they can make a trapezoid and parallelogram.

- Tell the children that they are going to have a chance to be puzzle designers. Have the children make their designs on standard size paper. When they complete a design that they like, the teacher should draw an outline around their creation on paper. (All pieces within the inside and outside of the puzzle could be outlined.) Some children may be able to sign their own names. Next write the name of the design on the front of the paper. Cover the finished product with clear contact paper and store in the manipulative center for future use.

Puzzle Pieces

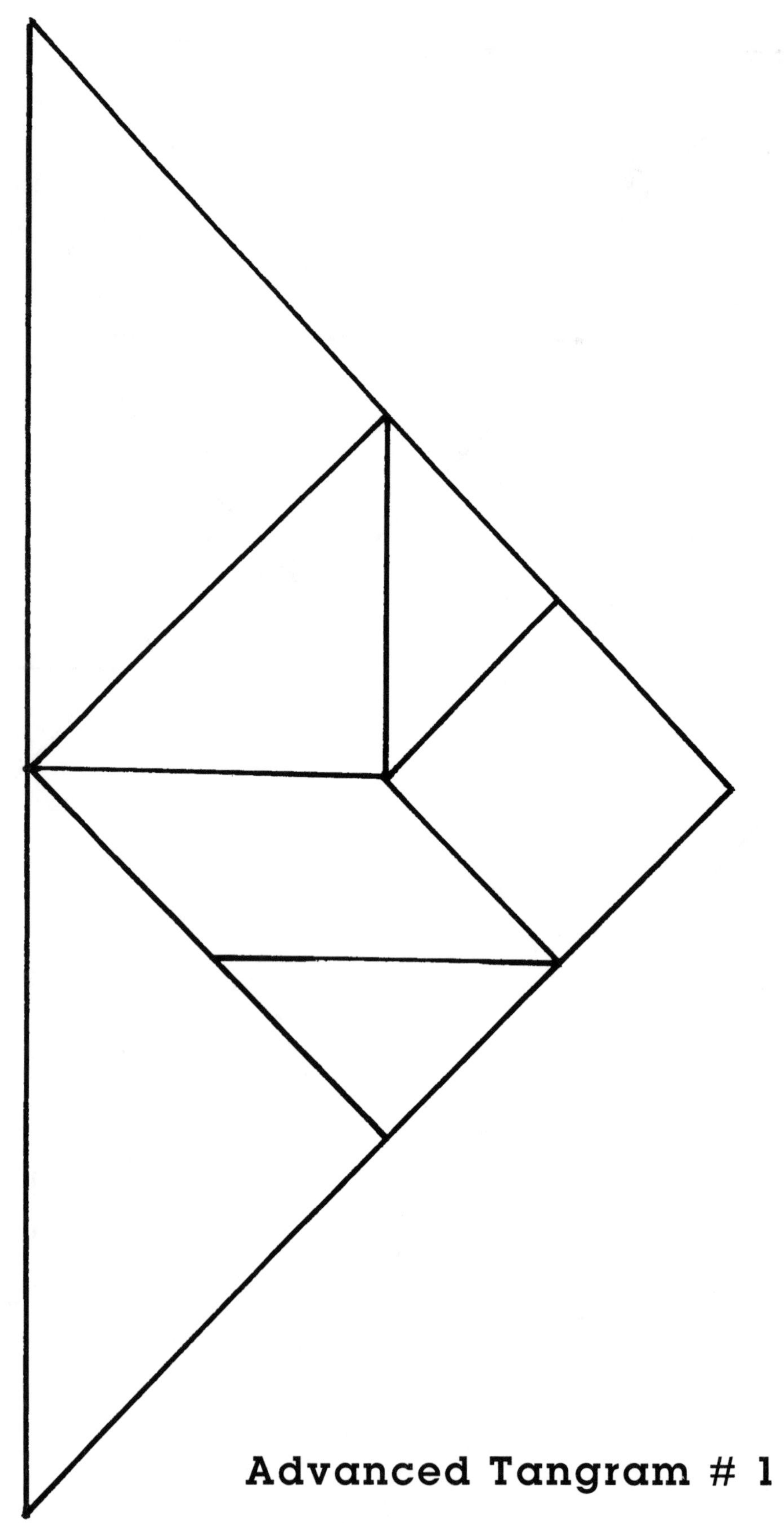

Advanced Tangram # 1

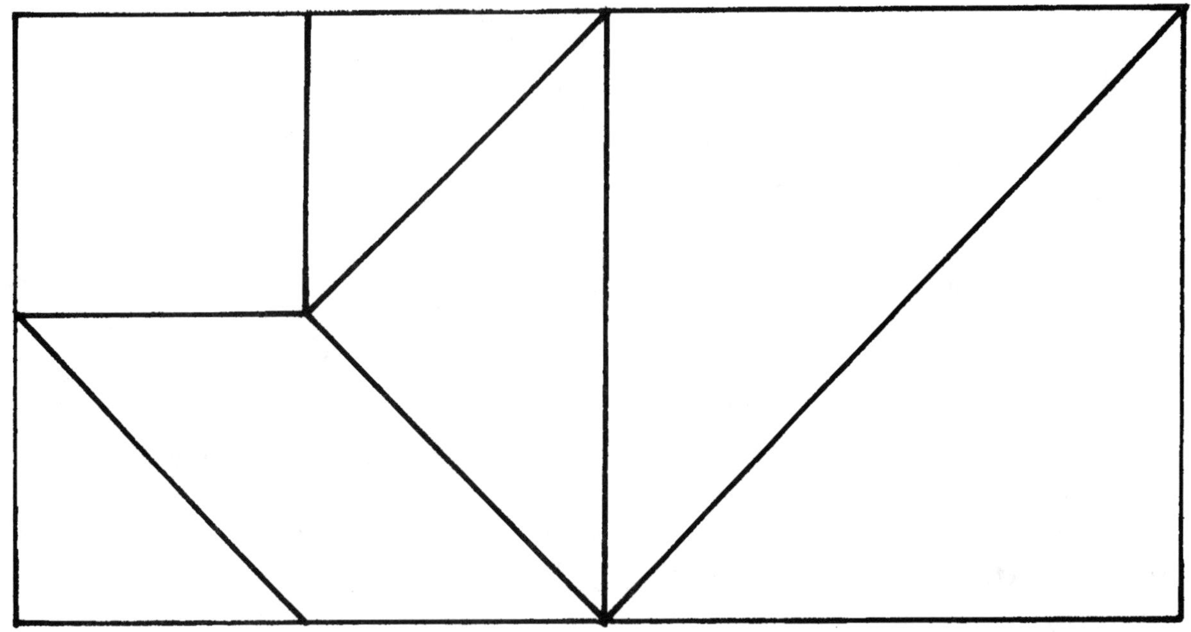

Advanced Tangram # 2

 to 

Sewing Cards and Dressing Boards

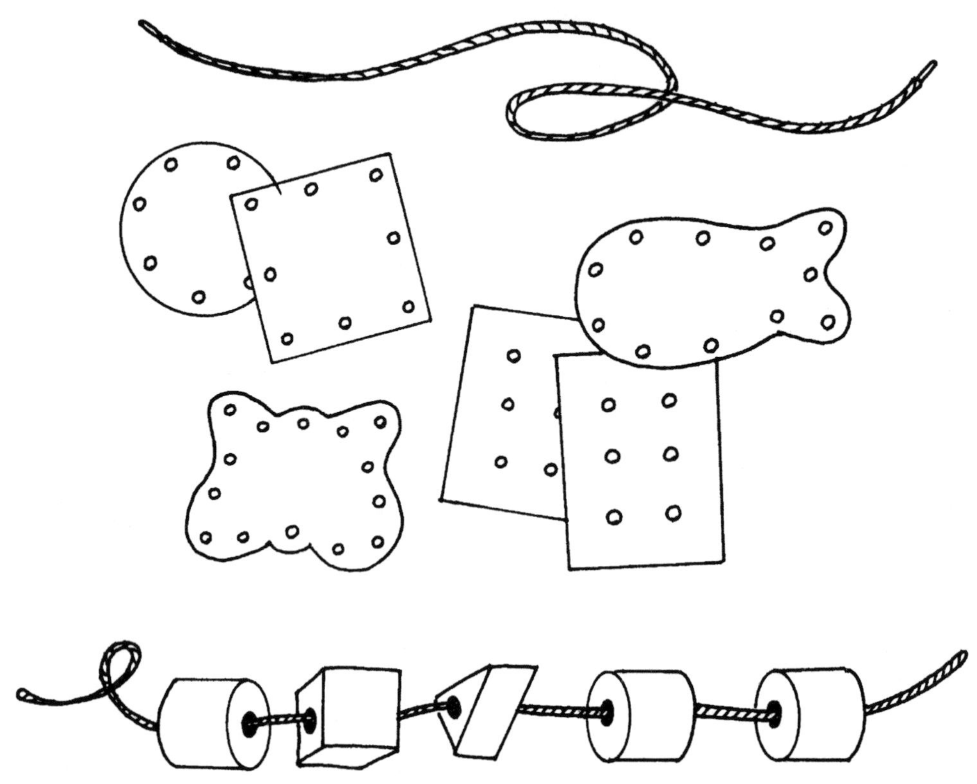

Purpose: This activity strengthens eye-hand coordination and provides practice with spatial relationships. It teaches essential dressing skills that contribute to a child's sense of independence and provides an awareness of how things fit together. It also provides fine motor practice as younger children learn fastening skills and older children practice tying.

Materials:

- heavy cardboard
- cord or old shoe laces
- old clothing with different types of fasteners
- scissors
- wooden beads
- wooden boards
- hammer and nails or stapler

HOME CONNECTION

Remind parents that developing skills that help the child become more independent is an important goal of early childhood. Showing children how to dress themselves and allowing them time to do so may demand extra time and patience, but the results are worth it.

Preparation:

1. Sewing cards are made by cutting heavy cardboard into 7 cm. x 12 cm. cards and punching or drilling holes in them. Sewing cards can also be made in different shapes. Collect shoe laces or cord for sewing.

2. Dressing boards are made from wooden boards. Use 6 boards about 22 cm. x 30 cm. each.

3. Find old clothing with a zipper, a button and buttonhole, a buckle, a snap, a tie, and laces. Cut out each type of fastener, leaving enough fabric around the fastener so that the fabric can be attached to the board.

4. Staple or nail the pieces of fabric to the board.

Activity: With children who are 3 years of age, begin by stringing large wooden beads together. They can make their own necklaces or just enjoy stringing colored beads in a pattern.

The sewing cards and dressing boards should be placed in the manipulatives center where children can experience them at their own pace. An observant teacher will provide assistance as it is needed and reinforce the skill with new vocabulary words, such as *button*: "You are able to button this. Where else do you see buttons? Can you button your sweater?"

Extensions and variations:

- Be sure to include dress-up props for both boys and girls that give practice with buckles, buttons, and zippers.

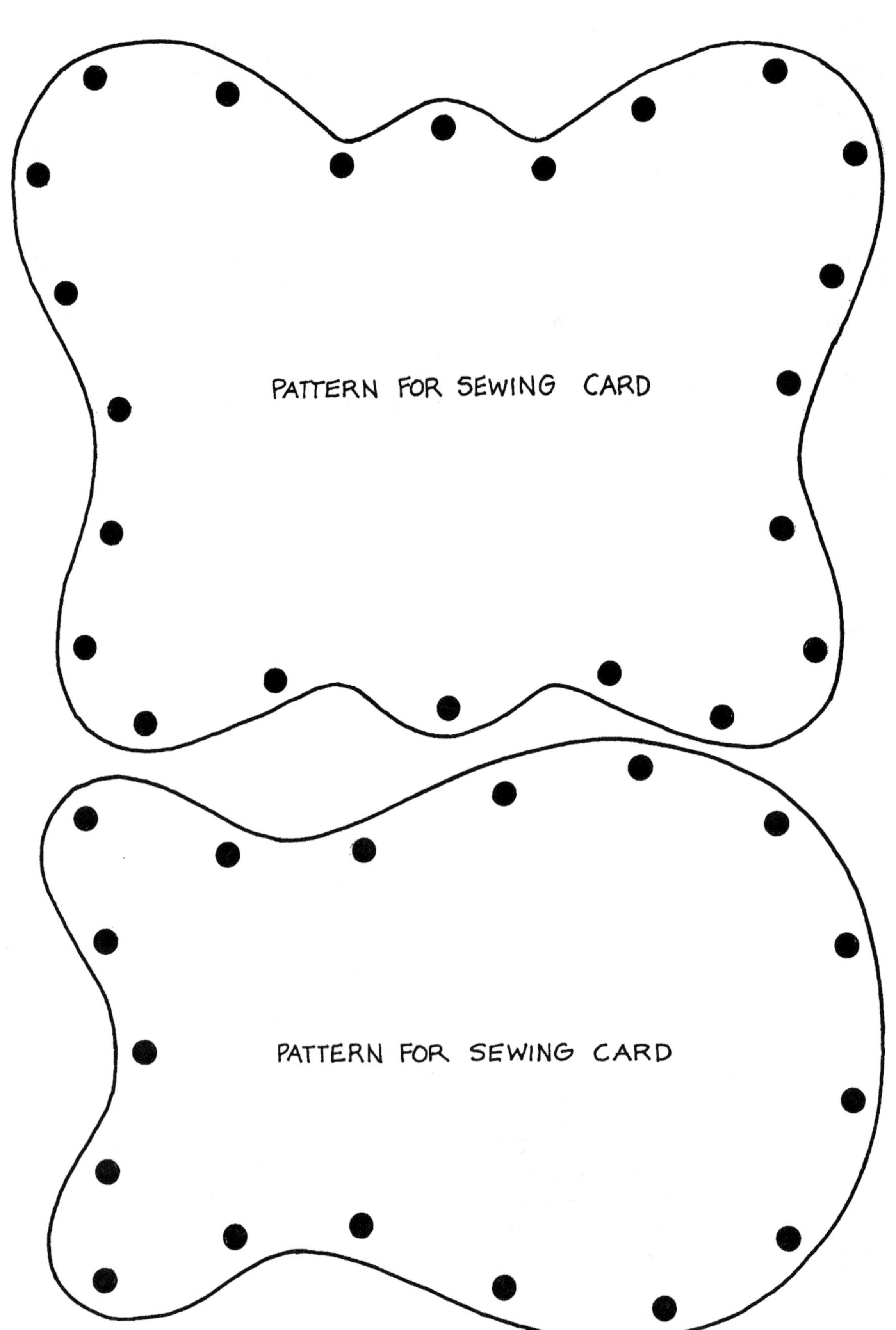
PATTERN FOR SEWING CARD
PATTERN FOR SEWING CARD

SCIENCE

Magnets: Yes or No

 to 

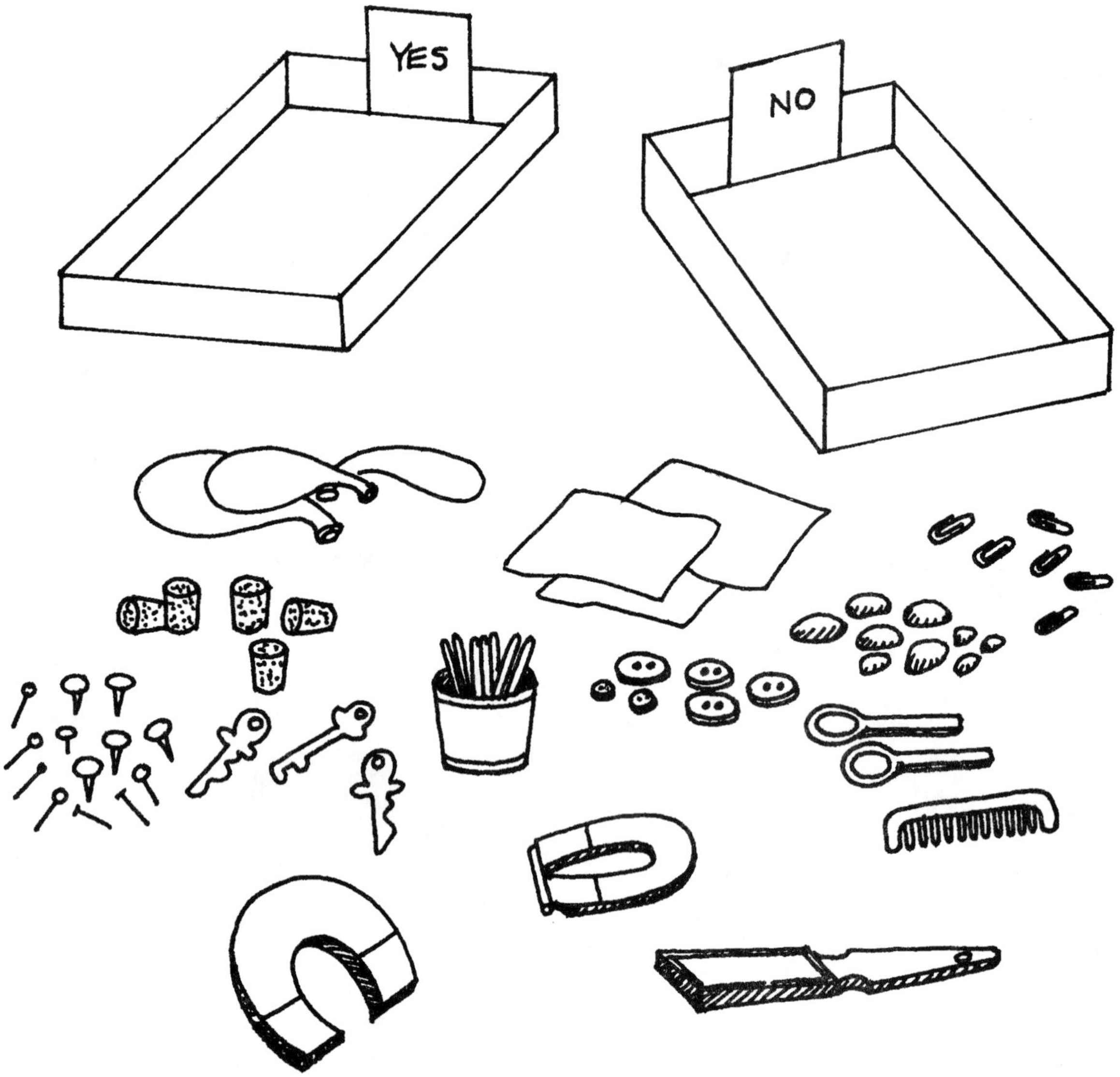

Purpose: This sorting and classifying activity expands a child's understanding of the concept of magnetism. Through active exploration with a magnet and objects, children will discover that magnets attract some objects, but not others. As children make predictions, test predictions, observe the results, and draw conclusions, they begin to practice scientific inquiry and discovery.

Materials: Collect a variety of items for experimentation—some that the magnet will pick up and others that it will not. Some examples of familiar objects are:

corks
coins
a metal spoon
rubber bands
rocks
keys
sticks
buttons
bottle caps
metal clips and fasteners

Also needed:
magnets
2 cards
2 trays or sturdy paper plates

Preparation:

1. Tape a card that is marked "yes" onto one tray or sturdy paper plate and a card that is marked "no" onto another tray or sturdy paper plate.

Activity: Children (especially the young) need time on their own for exploration and discovery. They will soon discover that the magnet picks up some items and will not pick up others. As the child begins to verbalize the concept, the teacher may support the play by providing "yes" or "no" trays for sorting the objects.

Later, with a new selection of objects, the children may be able to make predictions about whether the item will attract the magnet (yes) or not (no). After the child has made a prediction, test the object by sliding a magnet toward it.

Extensions and variations:

- Use drama to enhance this experience. Assign a child the role of a magnet and another child the role of a nail. If the magnet sticks to the object, ask the children to hold hands. Children will not easily tire of being magnets or magnetic and non-magnetic objects. This is a good game to assess the children's understanding of things attracted or not attracted by a magnet.

 to 

Exploring Magnetism

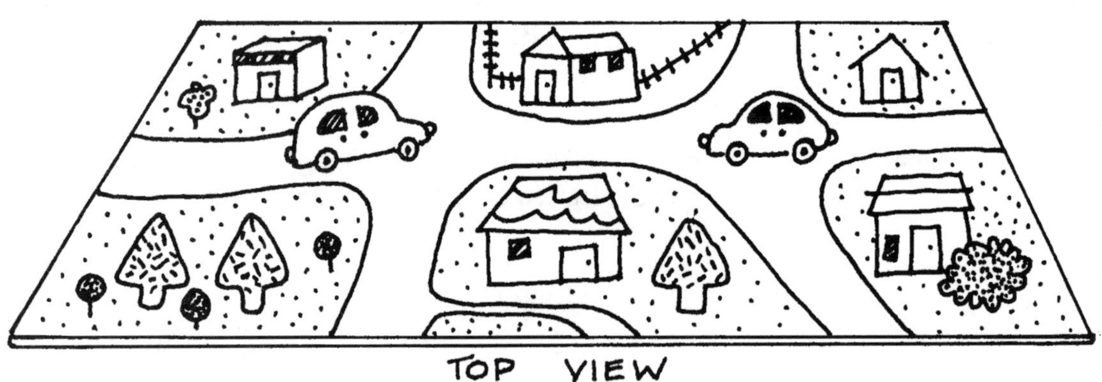

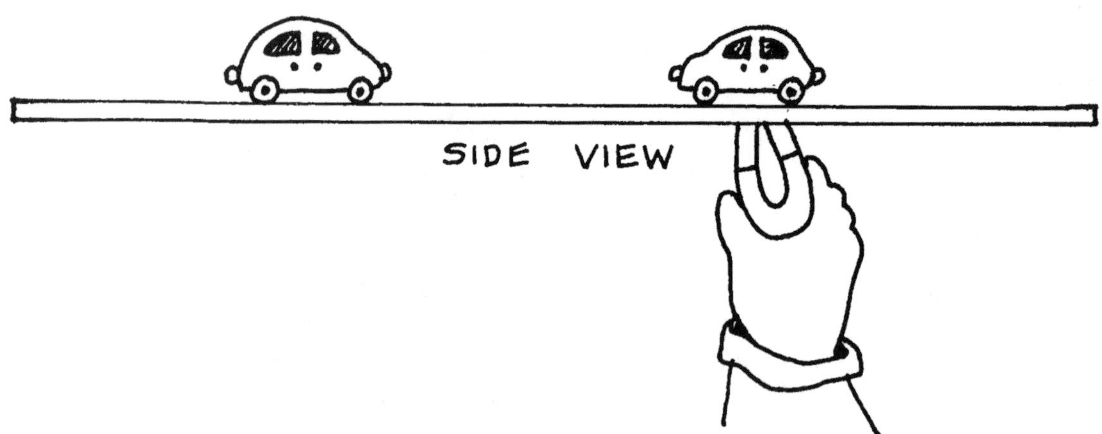

HOME CONNECTION

Suggest that parents make a magnet available to their child at home, if possible. Using the magnet, the child can go on a "magnet hunt" around the home to determine what materials are attracted to magnets. Remind parents that this should be approached as a game and children should be free to explore and experiment.

Purpose: As children investigate magnets and the concept of magnetism, they begin to realize that a magnet can affect an object. While magnetic attraction cannot be seen or felt, it effects can be seen and felt. Through participation in this activity, children experiment with familiar objects to see what things magnets attract (stick to).

Materials: small cardboard or plastic boxes
metal objects: paper clips, nails, screws, bolts, etc.
3 - 4 magnets

Preparation:

1. Collect small boxes made of cardboard or plastic.

2. Place familiar metal objects in the boxes, including paper clips, nails, washers, screws, bolts, etc.

3. Have at least 3 or 4 magnets available for each small group.

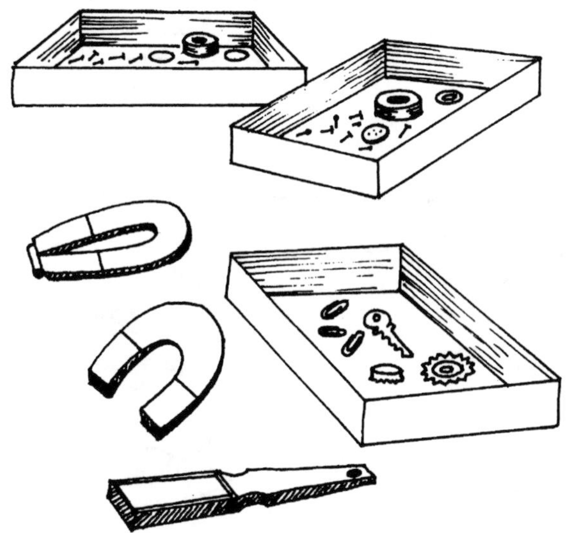

Activity: Begin magnet exploration by offering each child in the small group one magnet and a box containing metal objects. Permit the children to play with the magnets and objects. Listen carefully to their comments and watch the children's reactions as they share their ideas and discoveries.

The teacher can guide the exploration by sliding a magnet toward a paper clip. Ask the children to watch. What happens?

Extensions and variations:

- For 4 year old children, draw a city, including a network of streets. Small model cars, made of metal or with metal glued to the bottom, can be directed along the road network by moving a magnet underneath the paper.

- Magnetic attractions are part of this art activity. (Use small boxes to confine the activity.) Cut paper to fit inside the bottom of the box. Drip several drops of paint on the paper. Put a small metal object, such as a paper clip, on the paint drops. Slide the magnet underneath the bottom of the box and create a design. For variety, change objects or add another color of paint.

Sink/Float

Purpose: Experimenting with sinking and floating objects in water introduces scientific concepts of buoyancy, displacement, surface tension, density, and compression. Though these are sophisticated concepts, exposure to them at an early age facilitates understanding in later development. Through their experiments, children discover that some objects float and others sink. They compare and experiment with objects varying in size, shape, and dimension. Later, they make predictions based on their experiences and begin to draw some conclusions from their results.

Materials:

2 trays	water table, tub, or large container
cards	pencil or marker
water pitcher	

Sink/Float objects: corks, paper, leaves, plastic, metal, coins, rubber balloons, rocks, ice cubes, feathers, sponge, etc.

Preparation:

1. Place a water table, water tub, or large container in the room and put in it a variety of items that float and that do not float—for example, corks, paper, leaves, plastic, metal, rubber balloons, coins, rocks, ice cubes, feathers, empty and full containers, and a sponge. Other materials may be substituted.

2. Fill the water tub to about 10 cm.

3. You will need 2 trays for sorting the objects. Tape a card that is marked "float" on one tray and a card that is marked "sink" on the other.

Activity: Children 3 - 4 should be given many sensory-motor opportunities to explore water, something they enjoy doing very much. They discover, on their own, that some objects float and some sink.

A 5 or 6 year old (or a small group of children taking turns) can predict whether an object will float or sink and then place it in the water to test the prediction. After the object has been identified as one that floats or sinks, ask the children to place the object on the "float" or "sink" tray.

Extensions and variations:

- Teachers can encourage older children to select other objects from the room and predict whether these objects will sink or float.

- Have children experiment with a sinking object to make it float. How can it be changed?

- Have a scale available to weigh objects before placing them in the water. What conclusions can be drawn? Do similar objects that weigh the same both float?

- Add salt to the water and test the objects you tried in plain water. What floats in salt water? What sinks in salt water? Do any objects that float in salt water sink in plain water?

 to 

PAPER FUNNEL

CUT LINE

CUT HERE

CUT HERE

SODA BOTTLE FUNNEL

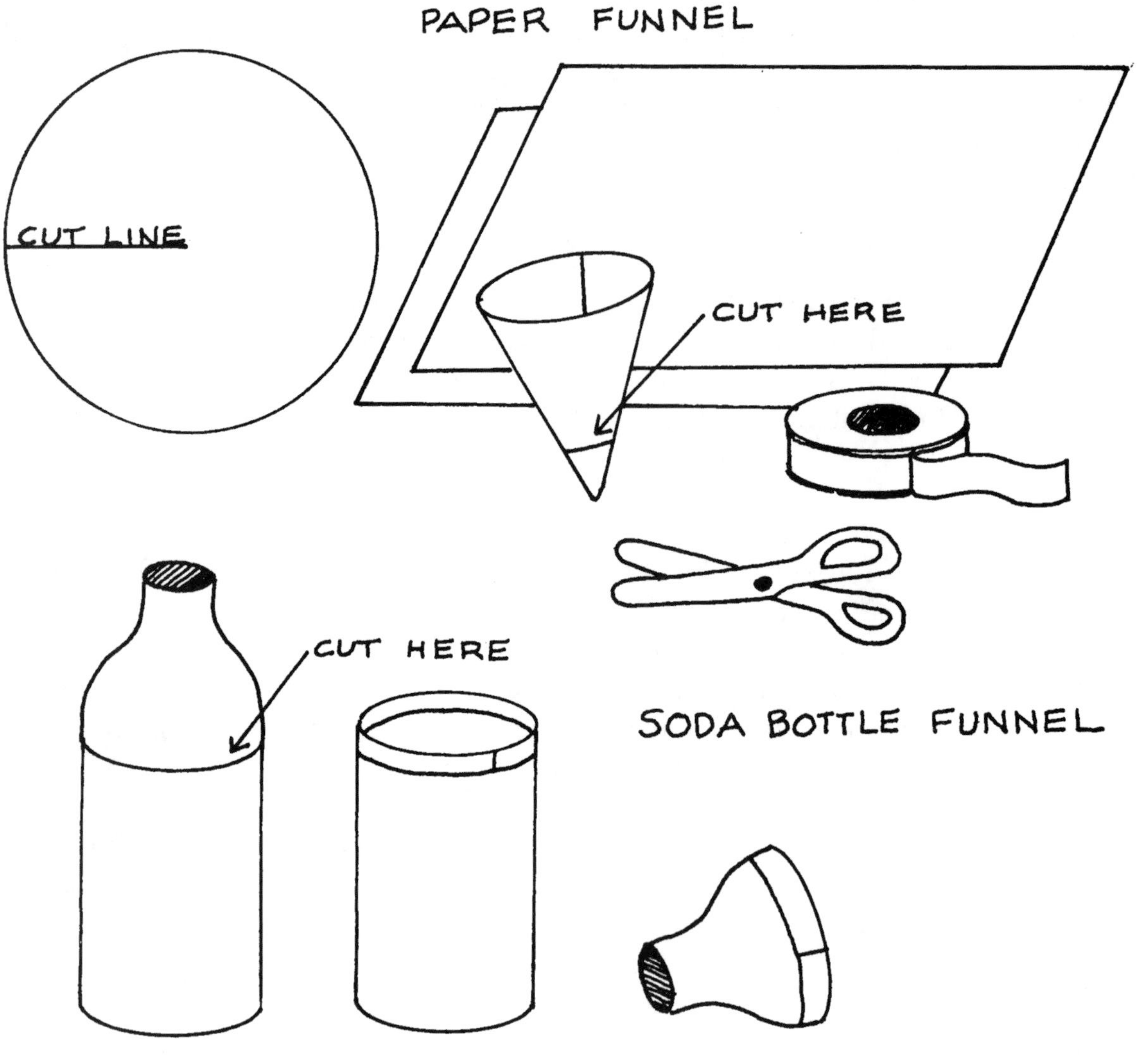

HOME CONNECTION

Parents can set up a supervised water play area at the kitchen sink or in the bath. Provide children with some containers for play.

Purpose: This activity helps children learn about measuring. Teachers facilitate water play by the selection of objects placed in or near the water table. Children begin to understand the concept of volume (that smaller parts or units fill up a larger container) as they pour cup after cup into the container. Children will also refine their fine motor skills and eye-hand coordination during the pouring process. Through the use of funnels, children learn the advantage of tools.

Materials:

- water table
- scissors
- transparent plastic soda bottles: small, medium, large (some to be cut in half to make funnels and containers; some to be used to pour water into)

Preparation:

1. Make funnels and containers by cutting plastic soda bottles in half. Tape the sharp edges.

2. Place the empty containers by the water table for the children to play with.

Activity: Teachers will want to give children, especially 3 year olds, many opportunities for water play before embarking on this measurement activity. Ask a child to select one of the smaller containers. Then offer the child a funnel to place over the opening of a plastic soda bottle. To guide the pouring experience, the teacher asks questions such as, "How many of these little containers of water fill up the soda bottle?" "What will happen if we use a smaller container to pour the water into the bottle?"

Extensions and variations:

- Children can compare their water measurement experiences with similar activities in the sandbox.

- Teachers can make funnels out of a cone-shaped paper cup or from a cut circle of paper. Cut a slit from the edge of the circle to the center. Take one edge of the slit and roll it up to form a cone. Staple, tape, or glue it in place. Snip off a small piece of the tip to make a hole.

- Select 2 containers of identical volume but different shapes (a short, fat one and a tall, thin one). Ask the children which container holds more. Then test the hypothesis and see the surprising result.

Soluable Substances

 to 

HOME CONNECTION

Parents from an apartment house or neighborhood can contribute old pots, cups, containers, and other utensils to provide shared resources for children's play with sand and water. They can also contribute extra potting soil or other substances that the children can experiment with.

Purpose: Water dissolves some substances, but others are insoluble. In this experiment, children will find out which substances dissolve and which do not. Much of cooking involves the concept of mixing substances together. Children will get a close look at several substances and, through discovery, begin to draw conclusions about their properties.

Materials:

- newspaper
- water pitcher
- salt, sugar, sand, etc.
- spoons
- pencil or marker
- cups of water
- stirrers
- bowls
- chart paper

Preparation:

1. Spread newspaper over a table top. Work with small groups of children.

2. Place 3 cups of water (or more if using more substances than salt, sugar, and sand) and stirrers before each child. Older children can pour their own cups of water.

3. Select a number of substances: salt, sugar, sand, etc. Place these substances in separate bowls with spoons readily available for scooping.

4. To help children organize their information, make a simple chart. List substances on one side and categories of soluble and insoluble as headings.

Activity: "Let's see what happens when we add a little salt in one of the cups. Stir it. Can you see it? Where is it? You can dip your finger in the cup and taste it. What do you taste? It is so small you can not see it has *dissolved.*"

Repeat this process using sugar, sand, etc. Use the chart to record the observations. After all children have had a turn, lead a discussion in a large group to draw conclusions.

Extensions and variations:

- A great extension to this activity is mixing oil and water. Children will learn more about soluble and insoluble materials in water.

Experiment with Sponges

 to 

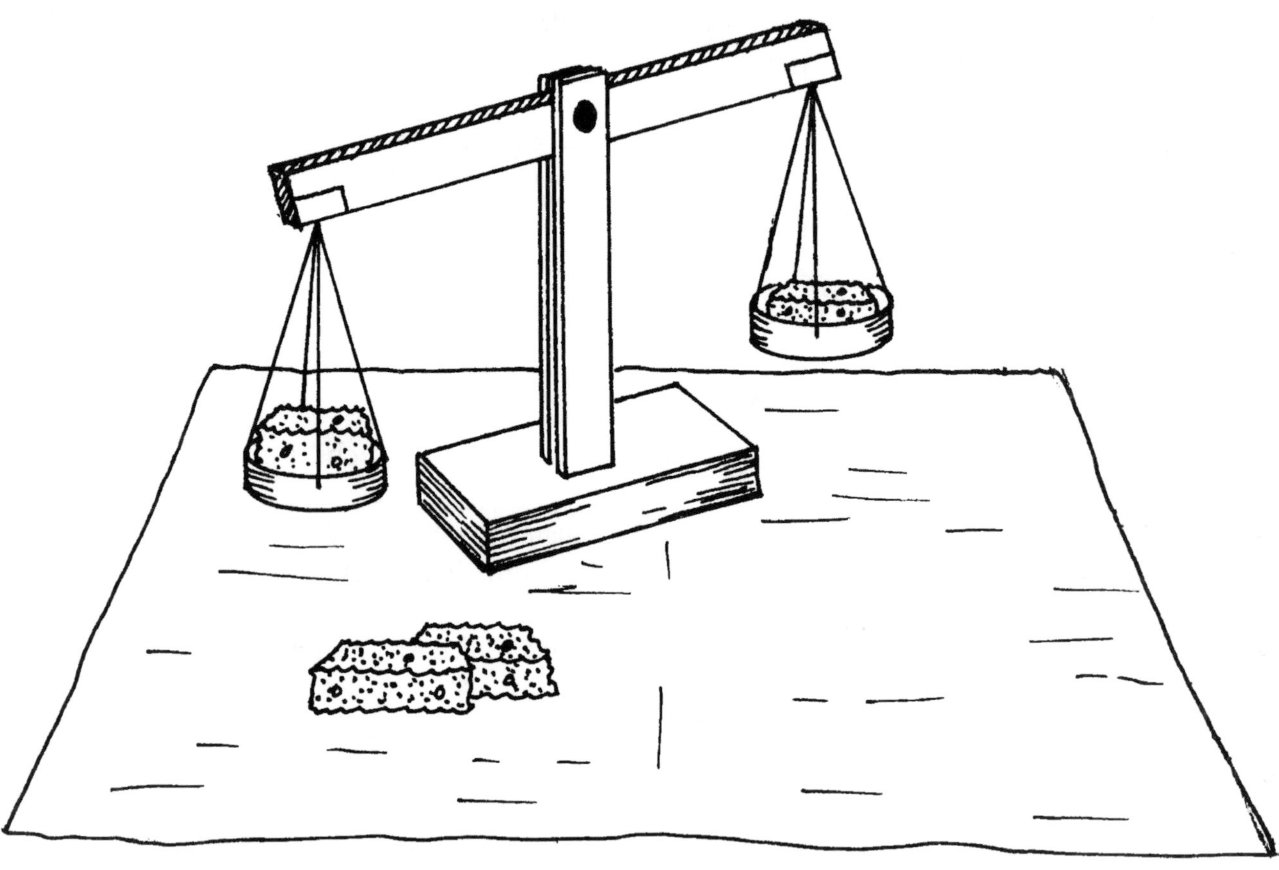

HOME CONNECTION

Parents, encourage children to help with the laundry! By handing their wet clothes to you as you hang them on the line, children will become aware of the difference in weight between clothes when they are wet and dry. By asking thoughtful questions to prompt the child to wonder why this difference exists, or what makes the difference, you turn a daily routine into an opportunity for discovery.

Purpose: In this water play activity, children make the discovery that water has weight. A water-saturated sponge will weigh more than a dry sponge. When expanding this experience, children will learn that the weight of any material increases when water is added to it. Furthermore, measurement is a mathematical skill, and this activity will further develop a child's understanding of weight.

Materials:

- newspaper
- sponges (same sizes)
- kitchen scale or balance
- water pitcher

Preparation:

1. Spread newspaper over a table top.
2. Place a scale near the water table.

Activity: Gather a small group of children around a water table or tub of water with a scale or balance nearby. "What does a scale do? Let's see what happens when we put a dry sponge on the scale. Now wet the sponge well with water and weigh it. Which is heavier, a dry sponge or a wet sponge? Why?"

Extensions and variations:

- Leave a wet sponge out overnight. Examine the sponge with the children during morning meeting. How has it changed? This extension naturally lends itself to the water painting activity (see page 170).
- With small groups of children, distribute a piece of wax paper, paper towel, and newspaper. Have children place a drop of water in the middle of each kind of paper. They will see that water spreads in different ways on different kinds of paper. Some kinds of paper absorb water faster and better than others. They will also see that the wax paper does not soak up water. Try this activity with scraps of different fabrics.

Exploring with Different Size and Shape Magnets

 to 

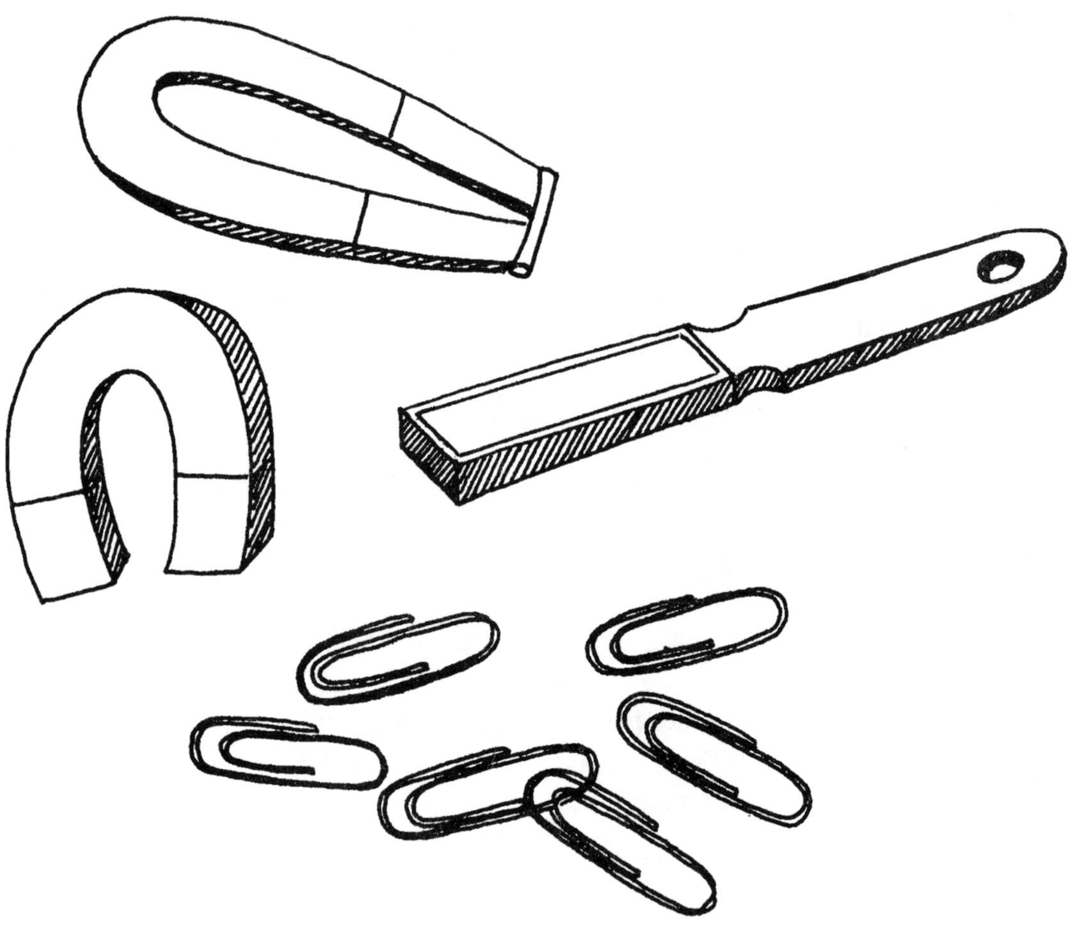

HOME CONNECTION

Arrange to have magnets available for a child to borrow from the classroom for a day or two at home. Each parent can sign out a magnet set for a specific time so that all children will have a chance to use the magnets at home. Explain that this process depends on families returning the magnets on time, so the next child who has signed up will get a turn.

Purpose: In this activity children investigate the properties of magnets. When they explore where magnets are most powerful, they begin to learn the principles of polarity and how magnets work. Children see that magnets come in many different shapes, sizes, and strengths.

Materials: paper clips
3 magnets of different sizes and shapes

Preparation:
1. Put out paper clips and magnets on the table.

Activity: This is a small group activity, designed for 2 or 3 children who will take turns sharing the different magnets. Ask the children to hold the curved end of the horseshoe magnet over a small pile of paper clips. Now ask the children to hold the ends of the magnet over the paper clips. Try this with the rectangular magnet. Ask children to discuss their findings (the ends of the magnet will attract the paper clips). Next work with a round magnet. Are the results the same or different?

Extensions and variations:

- Use a chain of paper clips to demonstrate the strength of the magnets' ends or poles. How many paper clips will the magnet attract? Are bigger magnets stronger than smaller magnets?

- Go on a magnet hunt in search of items that stick to a magnet. Notice where the items stick to the magnets.

Water Drop Slide

Submitted by Step by Step Bulgaria

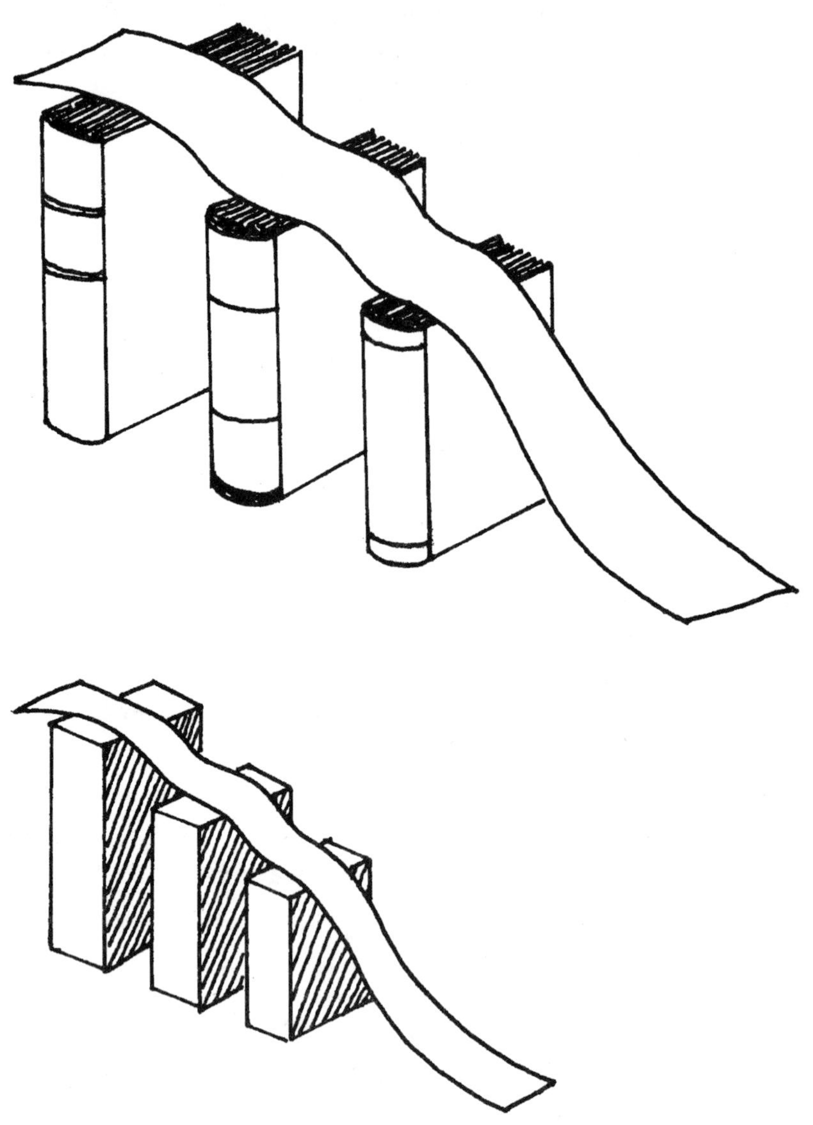

HOME CONNECTION

Suggest to the children that they set up a similar ramp at home and use a ball to show their families the game. First, have their parents predict how far the ball will roll from each point on the ramp, then test the hypothesis to see the results!

Purpose: This activity demonstrates that any object with weight, when dropped onto a hill or inclined ramp, will roll a distance that is in proportion to the height of the hill or ramp. This activity also helps children generalize the concepts of gravity, weight, speed, and distance from the inclined plane activity on page 192.

Materials:

- books
- water
- smooth plastic band
- tape
- dropper

Preparation:

1. The teacher should gather 3 books of varying height. Place the books at a distance from each other from tallest to shortest.

2. Cover the books with a smooth plastic band, and tape one end to the tallest book and the other end to the floor beyond the shortest book.

Activity: If possible, take the class outside to climb a hill and run down. If this is not possible, have the children remember a time when they ran up and down a big hill. Ask the class questions such as, "How did you feel when you climbed up the hill? How did you feel when you went down the hill? Which is easier, going up or going down?"

After thinking about their experiences playing on hills, children will work in groups of 3 to experiment with the water drop slide. Tell the children the water drop slide will be a make-believe hill. One child can start a drop from the highest book and mark the spot where the drop hits the floor. The next child starts the drop from the middle book, once again marking the spot where the drop hits the floor. Finally the third child can start the drop from the shortest book and mark the place where the drop hits the floor. Which drop went farther? Why? Did some drops travel faster than others? Which ones? Use these questions to promote ideas from the children. Have them suggest ways to test their ideas, or try the variations suggested below.

The drop rolls farther when it is started at the top of the make-believe hill than when it starts at a lower level.

Extensions and variations:

- Make a slide using stacked books and a wooden plank or thick paper. Release a small toy car from varying places on the slide. The steeper the slide, the farther a toy car will roll after it reaches the bottom.

- Go sledding with the children and apply the lesson of distance traveled on an inclined plane.

Creating Variations of Colors

 to 

HOME CONNECTION

Parents can do this activity with their children at home using glasses of water and food coloring. In doing so, they should use the time to become learners and explorers along with their children!

Purpose: This activity introduces the idea of changing color using a water medium. Children will see new colors form by mixing colors (for example, red and blue become purple). They can increase the intensity of color by adding more of the same color, or decrease the intensity by adding more water. Children identify and name colors such as red, orange, yellow, green, blue, and purple. This activity facilitates creative expression and exploration. The use of eye-droppers to mix colors also helps develop eye-hand coordination.

Materials:

- newspaper
- small plastic cups
- water pitcher
- red, blue, and yellow food coloring
- 3 eyedroppers
- straws or wooden stirrers

Preparation:

1. Spread newspaper over the table or on the floor.

2. Work in groups of 3 children. Provide each child in the group with red, blue, and yellow food coloring; an eyedropper; small cups half-filled with water; and straws or wooden stirrers.

3. At first, allow children to mix colors as they wish.

Activity: Tell the children that they will be investigators in this activity. Ask if anyone would like to guess what an investigator does. Discuss how an investigator solves problems and finds out how things change. Ask the children to discover new colors.

Extensions and variations:

- Instead of food coloring, children can use tempera paint in primary colors (red, yellow, blue) and secondary colors (purple, green, orange).

- Use larger containers for mixing. Many different colors can be created this way.

- Drop secondary colors on paper towels or coffee filters, demonstrating color separation. Ask children to observe what happens to the colors. (They will separate into primary colors!)

 to 

Fizz Surprise

HOME CONNECTION

When parents and children cook together at home, it is a perfect time to discover how materials mix and change. Young children can learn from their parents about the effect of liquids on dry materials if they have an opportunity to see what happens when these materials are combined. They also begin to realize that they can contribute to family routines.

Purpose: Fizz surprise is a science activity that introduces children to the idea that chemical changes occur when 2 materials are combined. Using the senses to explore the characteristics of vinegar and baking soda enhances a child's discovery of physical properties. (A gas is formed when the baking soda combines with the vinegar and expands.) As children make predictions and observations, they use scientific inquiry to answer questions.

Materials:

- vinegar
- baking soda
- black marker
- chart paper
- balloons
- small spoons
- transparent plastic soda bottle

Preparation:

1. Pour about 5 cm. of vinegar into a transparent plastic soda bottle.

2. Place 2 small spoonfuls of baking soda inside a balloon. A face can be added to the balloon with a permanent marker.

3. Put the neck of the balloon onto the open end of the bottle. Watch what happens!

Activity: Guide a small group of children through the task of adding vinegar to the soda bottle and baking soda to the balloon. Have the children smell each substance and ask if they want to taste either one. Ask children to predict what they think will happen if the balloon is connected to the bottle. Write their predictions on chart paper. Complete the experiment and record their discoveries on the chart. Can they guess why the balloon changed?

Over several days, give other groups the opportunity to experience the chemical changes by adding baking soda to the vinegar. If balloons are unavailable, add the baking soda to the vinegar in a glass jar or small dish. Record the observations.

Extensions and variations:

- Make a volcano by piling sand to form a mountain. Place the vinegar in a cup and insert it on the top of the sand mountain. Add baking soda.

- In a small group, review the sequence of the fizz surprise activity: "What happened first? What did we do next?" Then make a class book by writing each step on a page and asking the children to illustrate the pages.

- Have the children try to blow up a balloon. Demonstrate that when air is blown in a balloon it takes up space and the balloon expands. When the air comes out, the balloon deflates.

Marble Shoot

 to 

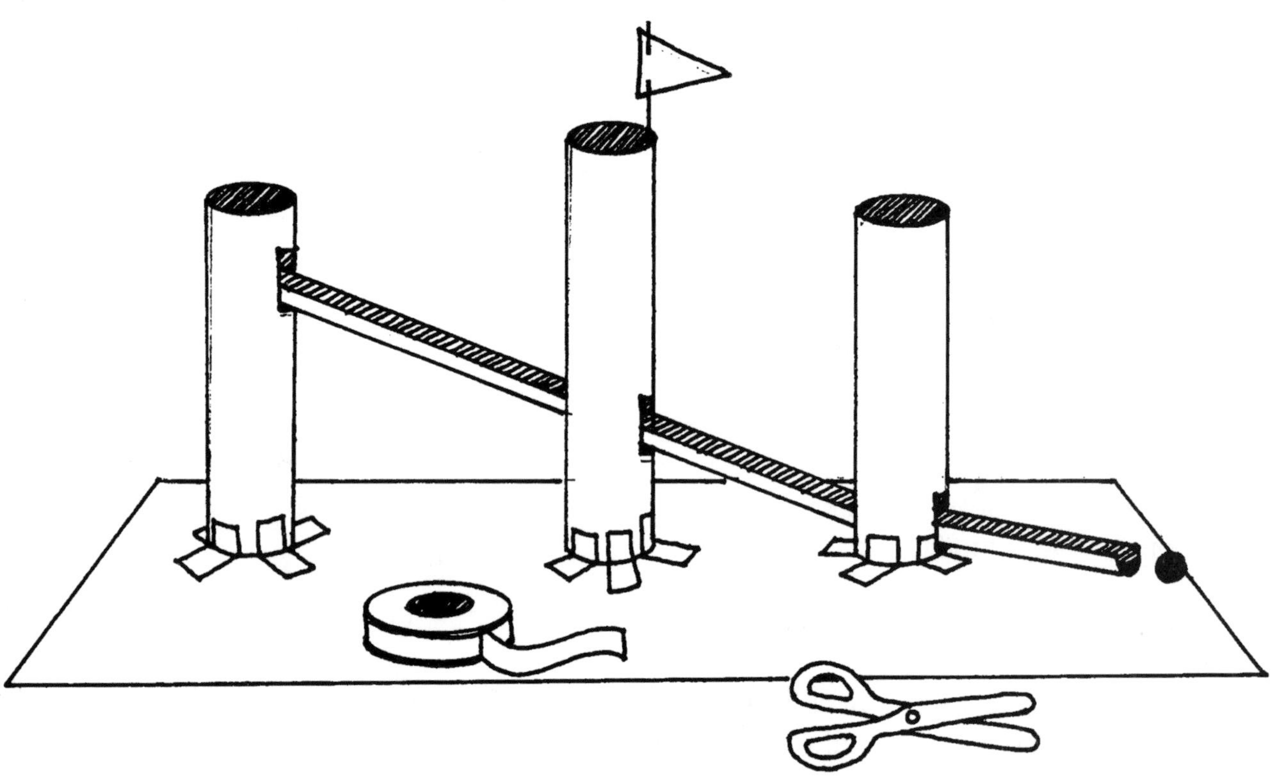

HOME CONNECTION

Collect paper tubes and paper food cartons from the recycling bins at school. Allow parents to take them home for children to build with at home. Ask parents to display the children's creations where they can be viewed by the family.

Purpose: In this activity, children drop a marble and let it roll through several bridging devices, traveling from the highest point to the lowest point of a "shoot" that they build from recycled materials. In the process they learn about the property of weight and the force of gravity upon an object. They also can experiment with variations in speed and distance traveled on inclined planes. The building exercise gives them experience with balance and weight in construction.

Materials: paper towel rolls, tape, marble

Preparation:
1. Set out the materials.
2. Cut some of the rolls in half the long way forming the "shoot" sections.
3. One finished marble shoot should be available for the children to see.

Activity: Gather 3 or 4 children together at a table and explain that each will be constructing a marble shoot. Begin by allowing the children to play with the marbles for a while. Roll a marble down a slide or inclined plane. "Which way does it travel?" "Can it go up the slide? Why? Can you feel its weight?" Explain that gravity causes objects to fall in a downward direction.

The teacher demonstrates that the marble is placed at the top-most part of the structure, shoots through it, and exits at the bottom, traveling a distance before it comes to a stop. The force of gravity pulls the marble toward the lowest point.

Then the children make their own marble shoots. Encourage each child to be creative, but be sure that the marble is always traveling in a downward direction. The teacher provides assistance as needed, especially cutting the openings in the tubes and attaching them with tape. The children will be delighted to see their inventions work. After several children have completed their marble shoots, compare the time it takes for the marbles to travel from start to finish. "Do the marbles travel faster down some structures than others? Why? Are some longer than others? Are some higher than others? How far does the marble travel when it exits different structures?" Place the marble shoots around the room for the children to see their creations.

Extensions and variations:
- Collect many kinds and varieties of recycled materials and let children make their own inventions: mouse traps, mazes, robots, space ships, etc. By using many materials, they begin to understand that both balance and stability are necessary for structures to stand.

- As a cooperative project, the children could make a class marble shoot.

SAND
AND
WATER

Soap Suds

3 to 5

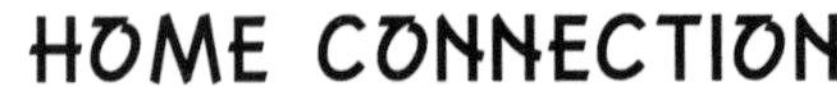

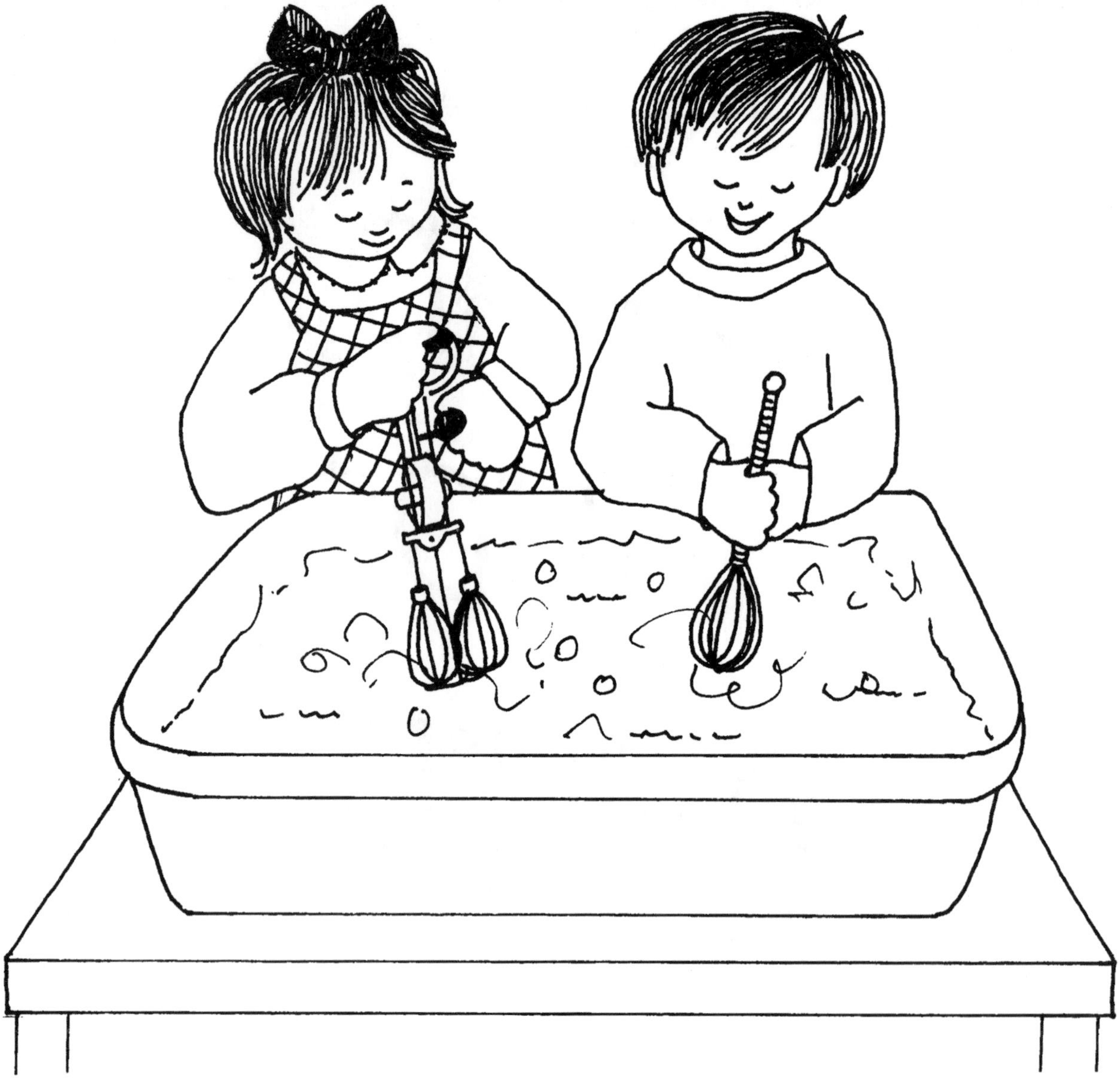

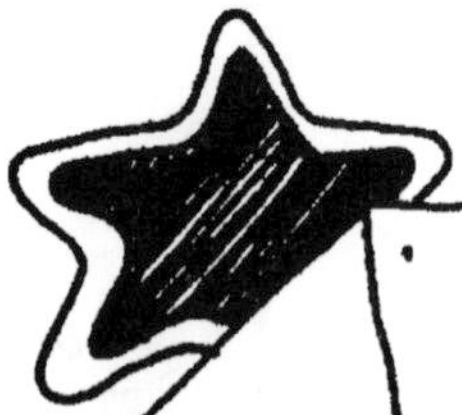

HOME CONNECTION

When children help with jobs at home such as washing dishes or wiping windows, they use the time and materials for exploration and play. Parents should know and accept this fact. They should allow children plenty of time for play and "messing about" before the job is completed.

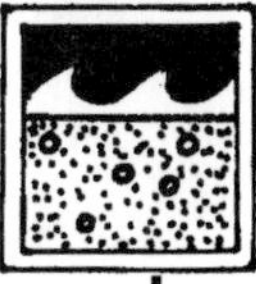

Purpose: Soap detergent added to water demonstrates a chemical reaction as the water composition changes. As children work, they learn the words for objects and find ways of describing the actions. While beating soap suds with a kitchen beater or wire whisk, the children sensorially experience making foam and bubbles and can communicate the findings. This activity refines hand coordination and small muscle control. It also helps some high-energy children to safely express their feelings.

Materials:

- water container or water table
- kitchen beater or wire whisk
- soap detergent
- water pitcher

Preparation:

1. Add a generous dash of soap detergent to the water table. Set a kitchen beater or whisk near the water table.

2. This activity is best done in groups of from 2 to 6 at the water table.

Activity: Observe the children as they explore water bubbles with a kitchen beater or wire whisk. Ask, "Are you making bubbles? Waves?" Ask them what happened to the soap detergent. They may say it's mixed with the water or it disappeared. Use the word *dissolve*. What kinds of words do the children use to tell what they are doing (*mix, beat, stir, combine,* etc.)? Bring the children together in a group and make a list of "words that tell what you do." In what other situations would we use these words? Examples are "mixing the batter to make a cake" and "beating an egg."

Extensions and variations:

- Children can help maintain a clean classroom. Have each child select an object to wash. This activity helps build responsibility in the classroom. "We all need to take care of our classroom and keep it neat and clean. Let's all help and wash a toy. We are all working together!"

Bubble Blowing

 to 

HOME CONNECTION

This is a simple activity to do at home. Copy the recipe and send it home with a note explaining that children can have fun and make interesting discoveries with a straw, bubbles, a cup, and time to play!

Purpose: Children use their senses to learn about physical properties. Blowing bubbles is a way to explore physical science. As water and detergent are mixed, children experience the change in chemical composition and enjoy the process. Rather than focusing on conclusions and results, bubble exploration helps to further develop their investigative skills.

Materials:

- liquid soap
- straws
- water pitcher
- scissors
- one 2-liter soda bottle
- water table or large pan or tub
- cups

Preparation:

1. In the water table or large pan or tub, mix the bubble solution according to the following recipe (children can help with the mixing):

   liquid soap
   water to fill 2-liter soda bottle

2. Cut straws in half.

3. Provide a cup partly filled with the bubble solution and a straw for each child.

Activity: Rather than directing this activity, have the children discover how to blow bubbles using the straws. Ask open-ended questions: "What is happening? What do you think is inside the bubble? Are there colors in the bubbles? What happens when the bubbles pop? What happens when you blow too hard? Too softly? If two friends blow a bubble to each other, do their bubbles connect?" Have a discussion about bubbles. Topics can include air inside the bubbles, shapes of bubbles, the outside "elastic skin" of the bubble, light rays and bubbles.

Extensions and variations:

- Have children blow air through a straw into plain water. Observe what happens to the bubbles. (They quickly break. The soap and water mixture makes bubbles that last longer.) Then blow into a cup of bubbles and notice what happens.

- Some children spontaneously blow a bubble toward another child. The child can catch the bubble on a straw, blow it back to the first child, and a game emerges.

- Dance like bubbles! Put on music and pretend you are a bubble with the children. Say, "Remember how the bubbles moved?" "Float gently through the air." "Did the bubbles make any sounds?"

Making and Using Sieves

 to 

Purpose: This activity demonstrates the effect of gravity on water. Using sieves, children learn that water flows downward seeking the lowest level and that it has weight. The children also learn the value of tools by making their own sieves.

Materials:

- plastic containers
- nails
- pitcher
- hammer
- newspapers
- small piece of wood

HOME CONNECTION

Suggest that parents spend time with their child doing something as simple as taking a walk in the rain together and noticing how the water is routed off buildings through gutters, downspouts, gargoyles, etc.

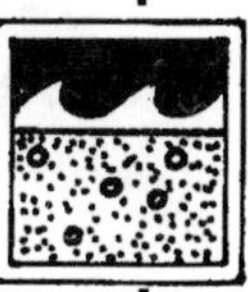

Preparation:

1. Collect a variety of discarded plastic containers, nails, and a hammer.

2. Cover the table with newspapers to avoid damage from the nails and to cushion the noise the hammers will make.

3. Provide ample adult supervision. The adults will need to use judgment as to whether the children can independently use a hammer and nails.

Activity: Invite 3 or 4 children, both boys and girls, to participate in the making of sieves. Ask each child to select a container and some nails. Tell them to turn the containers upside down and make holes in the bottom using the hammer and nails. Encourage the children to use different sized nails. Children can make as few or as many holes as they wish. (Placing a piece of wood under the container makes it easier to hammer.)

At the water table, ask, "What will happen if you put water into the sieve? In which direction does the water flow? What will happen if you raise your sieve? What will happen if you lower your sieve? From whose sieve is the water flowing fast? From whose sieve is the water flowing slowly? Why do you think this is? If you place a block under the sieve, what happens?" Encourage the children to try each other's sieves. They should also fill containers of different sizes with water. Ask, "Which containers feel heaviest? Why?"

Extensions and variations:

- Take a walk outside and discuss water flow patterns. "Will the water run up or down a hill? If it rains, what will happen to the water when it hits rocks, sand, soil?" Go outside when it rains and examine the water flow patterns. Were any of the class predictions accurate? Ask, "Where do the puddles form? Why?"

- With older children, discuss erosion. What effect does water runoff have on soil? How can the effects of water be minimized to lessen erosion?

 to 

Walnut Shell Boats

Purpose: Making sail boats promotes a further understanding of buoyancy and surface tension. (This activity extends the "sink-float" experiment.) Children begin to understand that there are certain conditions that allow for buoyancy.

Materials:

- walnut shells
- scissors
- small amount of clay
- water pitcher
- toothpicks
- crayons or markers
- water table, tub, or container
- small pieces of thick colored paper

HOME CONNECTION

An enjoyable way to introduce this activity is to invite families to come and help eat the nuts because the children need the shells for a project. (It is important to have plenty of walnuts!) Save the shells; if there are extra shells, send one home with each family so they can make a boat with their children.

Preparation:

1. The children cut out a variety of shapes (circles, rectangles, squares, triangles) about 7 - 8 cm. in height.

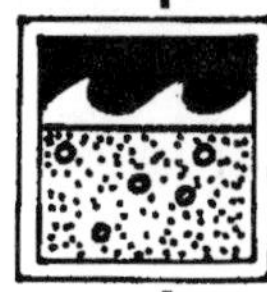

2. The children choose a shape for a sail and decorate the sail using crayons or markers.

3. Each child then takes a "pinch" of clay and presses it into a hollowed half of a walnut shell.

4. The teacher or adult helpers put the top portion of the toothpick through the sail, and the children can then secure the pointed bottom of the toothpick in the clay. The boat is ready to set sail!

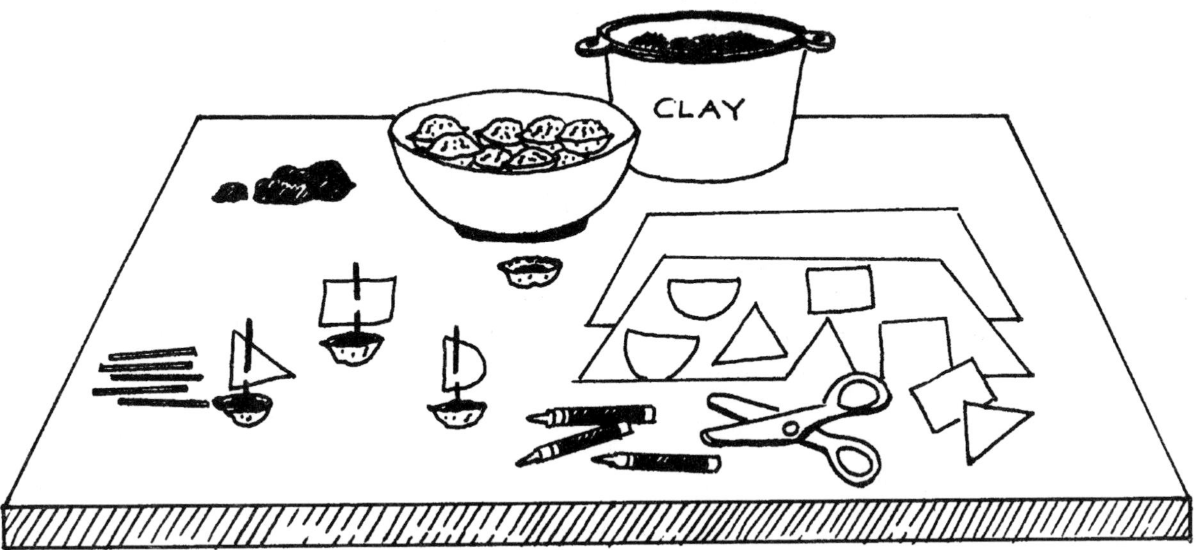

Activity: In a small group, the children place their boats in water and quietly observe them. Are they floating? Ask, "Have any sunk? Why do you think this happened? Why do the boats float? What happens if we make waves? Let's count the number of boats sailing in the water." Ask children to predict what happens when cargo is added to the boats. Then add pebbles, coins, or paper clips. "What happens to the boats?"

Extensions and variations:

- Water transportation is an appropriate theme to examine with young children. Begin a theme-related study about boats, ships, submarines, etc.

- Make boats out of other materials, such as milk cartons or Styrofoam. The following materials are good to have available: aluminum foil, clay, straws, and toothpicks. Attach decorations to the boat using glue, tape, or staples.

to

HOME CONNECTION

Parents and children can line themselves up in order of height, from smallest to tallest. Friends and relatives can be included to add to the fun! Each person makes a sound, from a low sound up to a high sound.

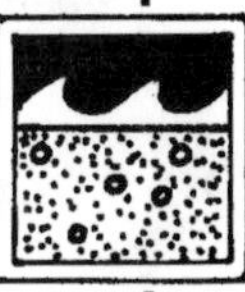

Purpose: Mathematics is an abstract system for organizing and ordering. Because young children think very concretely, concepts such as assigning quantity to numbers are most meaningful with many things to count and put in order. Ordination involves the ability to put things in order, recognizing a size pattern—for example, smallest to largest or least to most—and being able to reverse the pattern.

Materials:
water glasses of equal size
water pitcher
sand (optional)

Preparation:

1. Select 3 - 5 glasses or containers of equal size.
2. Fill glasses with water to varying levels.

Activity: By comparing the glasses of water on a table, the children will have an opportunity to order. Ask a child or a small group of children to order the glasses from most full to least full or least full to most full. Work from left to right. Encourage children's familiarity with mathematics vocabulary: *more, less, most, least.*

Extensions and variations:

- Sand could be used in the containers instead of water.
- Ask the child or children to order 3 measuring cups from smallest to largest.
- Ask the children to find other things in the room that can be ordered from largest to smallest.
- Fill 7 glasses with increasing amounts of water. Tap each glass and listen. How does the sound change?

Oil and Water

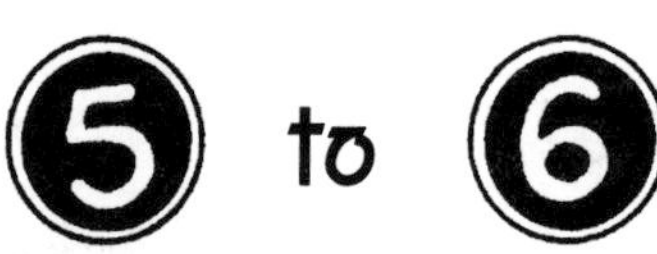

Purpose: When mixing water and oil, children will recognize how liquids of different densities interact. By being encouraged to describe what they see, they will come to understand the basic concepts of insolubility, density, and viscosity. As the children explore the notion of the insolubility of water and oil, they can think of liquids that *are* soluble in water. Using their senses, children will draw conclusions based on their observations, which is a prerequisite skill for using the scientific method.

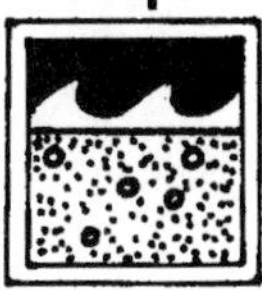

Materials:

funnel	water
water cups	measuring cup
vegetable oil	clear plastic soda bottle
large sheet of paper	pencil or marker

Preparation:

1. Preceding this activity, the class should experiment with (a) mixing sugar or salt in water (see page 82) and (b) adding soap detergent to the water table (see page 98).

2. Using a funnel, pour a cup of water into the bottle, then a cup of oil into the bottle.

Activity: Have a basin of water available. Gather the children and say, "Let's talk about water today. What do we know about it?" Try to elicit responses dealing with the physical properties of water (for example, it is wet). "Does it have a shape? A color?" Next use the word *liquid* to describe water. Ask, "Do you remember when we put soap detergent in the water? What happened?" "Yes, you're right. We made soap bubbles and foam. Remember, too, that the detergent disappeared, and I told you it had mixed with the water. We called that *dissolving.*" Write down the children's responses in their own words on a large sheet of paper.

Then announce, "Today we are going to conduct a different experiment with two liquids, water and oil." Pass around the cup of water and then the cup of oil. "How are water and oil the same?" "How are they different?" Write down all responses. "Watch carefully now! I'm going to put both into the bottle." Do so, and close the bottle cap firmly; pass the bottle around and ask the children, "What happened?" Wait until each child has seen the bottle, then ask, "Did the oil and water mix? If I shake the bottle will they mix?" Give each child an opportunity to shake the bottle and to get a close look at the liquids. Write down all their findings on a large sheet of paper.

Repeat the experiment with other small groups of children. Write down their observations also.

Bring all the children back to the large group to discuss their findings. Can some conclusions be drawn? Write the conclusions down. Display the papers with their responses and conclusions near the water and sand tables.

Extensions and variations:

- On another day, add other liquids to water and note if they dissolve or mix with the water.

- Try mixing other solids—such as salt, sugar, flour, or sand—with water. Do these solids dissolve?

DRAMATIC
PLAY

A Visit to the Post Office

 to 

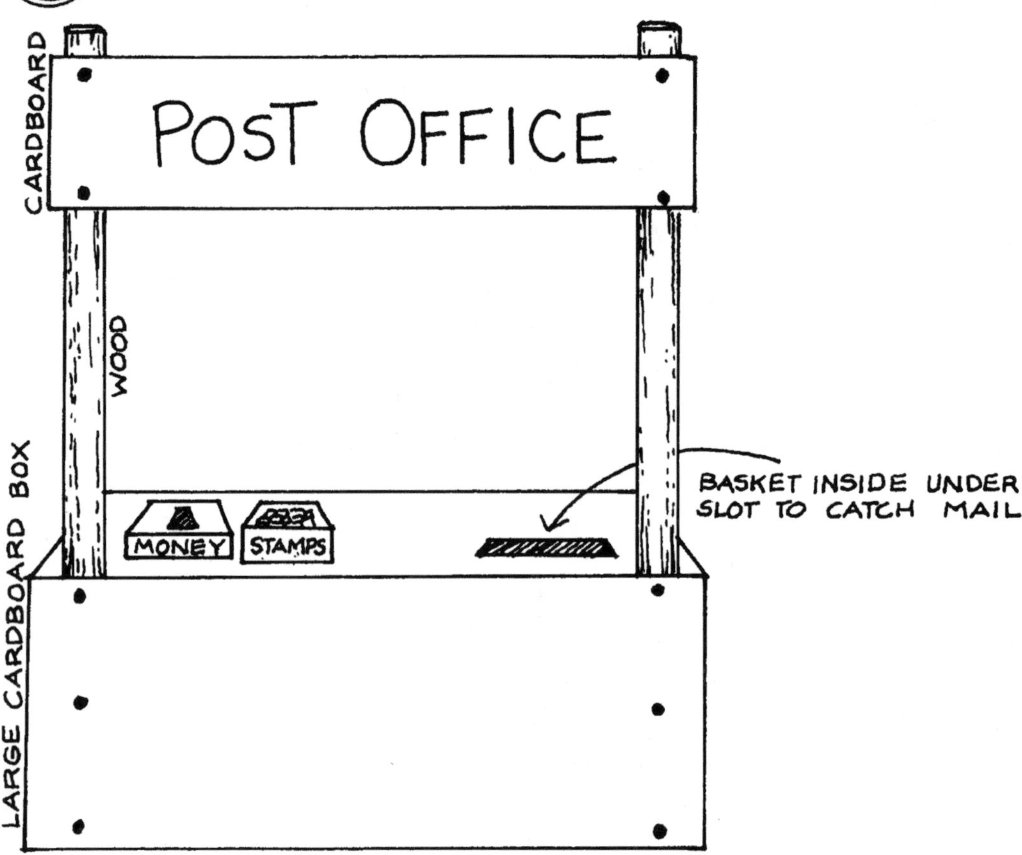

Purpose: There are many ways to nurture dramatic play. This activity uses a visit to the local post office as a good starting point for activities that foster both imagination and thinking. The visit demonstrates how math, social studies, science, and language are integrated into the workplace. The children see adults using skills in the professional world that they practice in the classroom, like sorting, counting, and using numbers. The experience involves the children in preparation for the visit and encourages both girls and boys to dramatize the roles seen on the visit.

HOME CONNECTION

Send a note home informing parents about the post office project. Ask for volunteers to accompany the class on the trip. Let the parents know that they will be receiving letters from their children. They should talk with the children about the post office trip and later let them know when the children's letters arrive.

Materials:

- crayons
- paper
- each child's address
- spools, buttons, or empty film canisters
- markers
- envelopes (one per child)
- enough coins per child to purchase a stamp

Preparation:

1. Teachers should make an appointment to see the person in charge of the post office to arrange for a visit. Ask that person if each child can have an opportunity to purchase a stamp, place it on his letter, and deposit it in the mail slot or box for outgoing mail. Also ask if it would be possible for the children to see how the mail is sorted and to hear how it gets delivered. Establish the date. Teachers should send a note home telling the parents of the planned visit.

2. Ask the children to make drawings or designs to send home to their parents.

Activity: This activity is divided into two parts—preparations before the trip and after the trip. Before the trip, teachers can tell the class that a trip to the post office has been arranged. In small groups, ask the children to each make a drawing or design (their "letters") that they will mail to their parents. (Or the teacher could write down messages or stories that the children would like to send home.) Help them fold their letters and put each one in an envelope. In the small groups, the teacher should show how she addresses each envelope with their addresses.

After the trip, be sure to have props available so that children can imaginatively play post office. Offer spools, buttons, or empty film canisters from the art center for the children to design their own stamps. Have children also make their own make-believe money so that they can buy or sell stamps, deposit money, and count the change. Encourage the assignment of roles as seen on the visit.

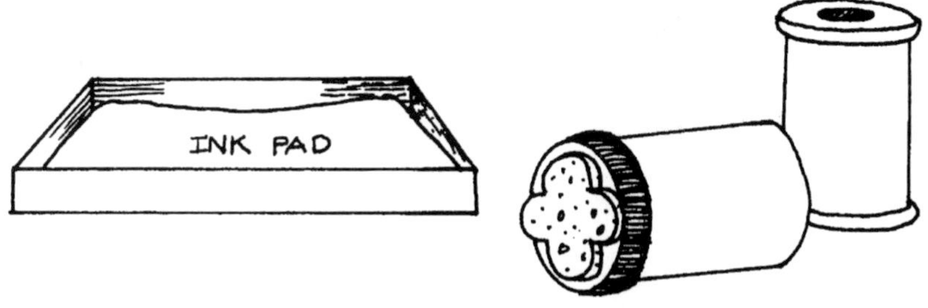

Extensions and variations:

- Arrange visits to a firehouse, a doctor's office, and a construction site.

- Visit a large food store. Notice how foods and other items are classified: dairy products, canned goods, soap products.

Tin-Can Telephones

 to 

HOME CONNECTION

Ask parent volunteers to prepare the cans ahead of time (clean them, poke a hole in the bottom of each can). This is a good way for parents who cannot come to school during the day to be involved in an activity. Other parents can come into the classroom and assist with helping to tie and assemble the "telephones." Explain to parents that their role is to help the children make the telephones, not to do it for them.

Purpose: The tin-can telephone really transmits sound. Although the scientific principles involved may be too abstract for the developmental level of young children, the tin-can telephone can enhance and extend children's language and play experiences. Through speaking, listening, and thinking, children express their individuality and creativity. The telephone offers children an element of reality in their play.

Materials:

- juice or aluminum cans
- a nail
- long string or fishing line
- masking tape

Preparation:

1. Cover all sharp edges of cans with masking tape.
2. Poke a hole in the center of the bottom of each can with a nail.
3. Thread string through each of the cans. Make a large knot in the string at the bottom of the cans.

Activity: Ask a pair of children how people can talk to each other when they cannot see one another and are far apart. Ask them if they have ever talked on a telephone. To whom did they talk? Show the children the tin-can telephone. Give one end to each child. Let them experiment with the telephone.

If, after trying it out, the children say the phone does not work, ask questions such as, "Are you talking right into the open end of the can?" "Are you listening through the open end of the can?" "Is the can really close to your ear?" "Maybe you are standing too close to each other. Can you try standing farther apart?" Have the other children make their telephones.

Extensions and variations:

- Once the children can operate the telephones easily, use them in dramatic play situations: "Where can we install our phone? Can we use our telephone to talk between activity areas?"
- Many activities can be planned that include the telephones. For example, use the phones to invite friends to a picnic. (Provide baskets, blanket, make-believe food, etc., for the picnic.) The telephones could also be used in the block corner to play "construction."

 to 

Binoculars

Submitted by Step by Step Hungary

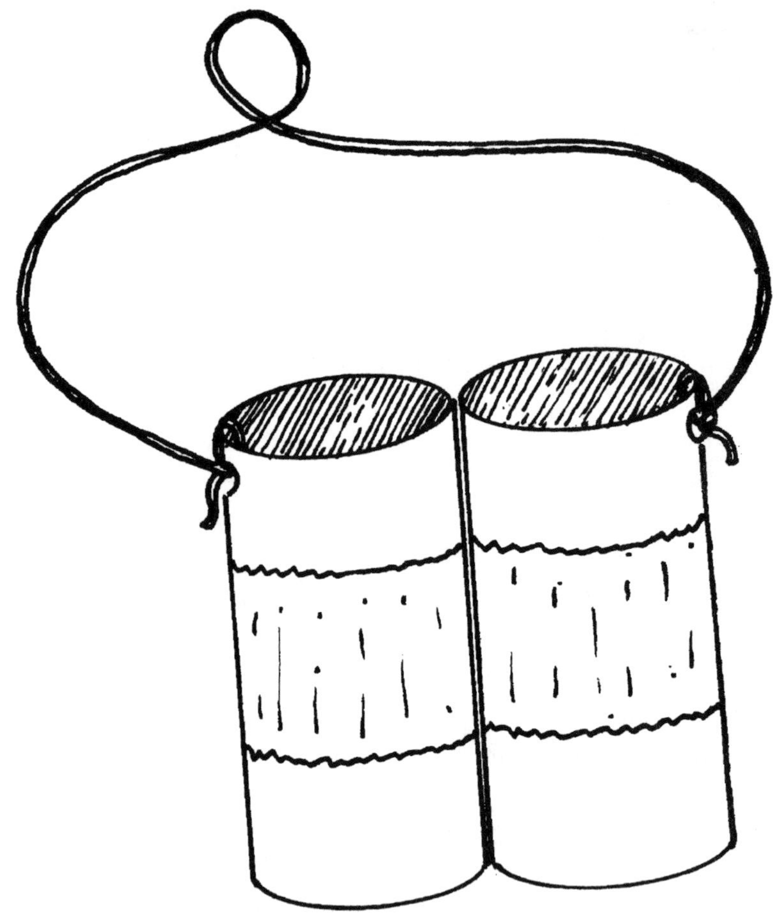

HOME CONNECTION

Attention all parents! Please save cardboard tubes and containers that can be used in our classroom projects. We will have a receptacle in the classroom for you to drop them off. Many thanks!

Purpose: This activity introduces the class to optical instruments that make distant objects appear nearer and larger. It encourages imagination as children recycle materials to create make-believe binoculars. Props such as this are designed to enliven children's play, often sustaining or extending it.

Materials:

2 toilet paper tubes for each child
colored tissue paper
glue
hole puncher
cords

Preparation:

1. Take 2 toilet paper tubes to make 1 pair of binoculars.
2. Cover the tubes with colored tissue paper. Glue them together vertically.
3. Punch a hole in each tube and attach a cord so that the binoculars can be worn around the neck.
4. Use the binoculars to show the children what they will be making.

Activity: Introduce this activity to children when they are engaged in play that is relevant. (In Hungary, the children were working with the theme of ships.) If possible, borrow real binoculars and give children a chance to try them. Explain how, why, and when they are used. Keep the explanations short. Then, invite a group of 4 children at a time to make their own binoculars. Encourage them to choose the color of tissue paper that they prefer to glue onto their binoculars. Help them attach the cords. The binoculars narrow the field of vision sufficiently to accentuate what is being observed.

Extensions and variations:

- Children can look at objects through a magnifying glass. They can easily compare the size of the object in their hands with its magnified self. Give the children many objects to magnify both indoors and outdoors. Try leaves, flowers, snowflakes, a feather. Such experiments help create a sense of wonder in children.
- If a microscope is available, let children look through it. Make the link between the binoculars, the magnifying glass, and the microscope. These are optical instruments. The microscope is used to see objects too small to be seen without special lenses.

 to 

Shadow Play

Purpose: Children enjoy playing with their shadows on the playground, creating puppet shadows on the wall, and guessing what an object is from its shadow. In this activity, children learn about the interaction of light, shadows, and distance. Shadow play also encourages creative expression.

HOME CONNECTION

Grandparents, other older relatives, and parents probably all played shadow games when they were children. Playing with shadows is a way for adults to share their childhood experiences with their children. Encourage parents to recognize opportunities for that kind of interaction.

Materials: flashlight or lamp
sheet

Preparation:

1. Hang a sheet in such a way that it hides the object that will create the shadow.

2. Have the flashlight or lamp readily available for shadow play.

Activity: With a small group, an interesting guessing game is to identify the shadows of known objects. From behind a sheet, shine a light on several types of fruits one at a time. Bananas, grapes, apples, and other fruits will puzzle the group as they try to guess the type of fruit and to figure out how they are appearing on the sheet.

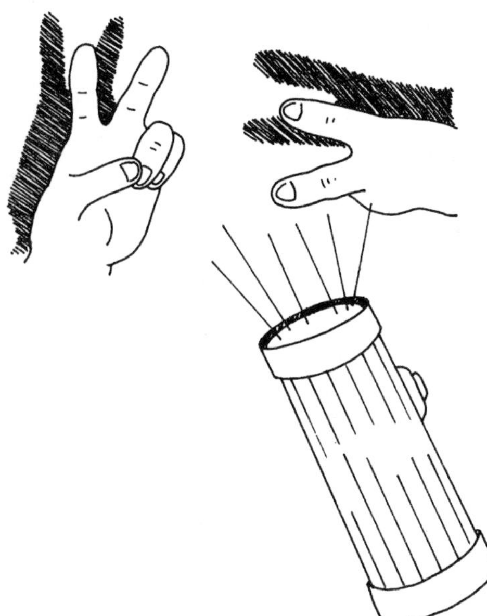

Then, again with a small group, shine a flashlight or other light source on a wall in the dramatic play area. Children use their fingers to produce shadow figures. They will enjoy making rabbit ears, a duck, a dog, a monster, or abstract forms. Children can also use puppets and the teacher can add music to allow for rhythmical movement and self-expression. Have the children move their puppets closer and farther from the light source and observe how the shadows change.

In a large group, perhaps outdoors, on a bright day, encourage the children to make silly movements and observe their own shadows. Teachers can introduce a quick "copy cat" (follow-the-leader) game: "Everybody jump! Everybody hop! Now, everybody dance!" This high-energy game will get the children up and moving.

Extensions and variations:

- On the playground, play a shadow touch game. Have the children in the group make one connecting shadow by having their shadows touch each other's. Then, play shadow tag.

- Cut paper shapes. Can children identify the shapes and any other characteristics about the shapes. How many sides does the triangle have? Can the children make the shadow of the shape get larger or smaller? How?

Megaphones

to

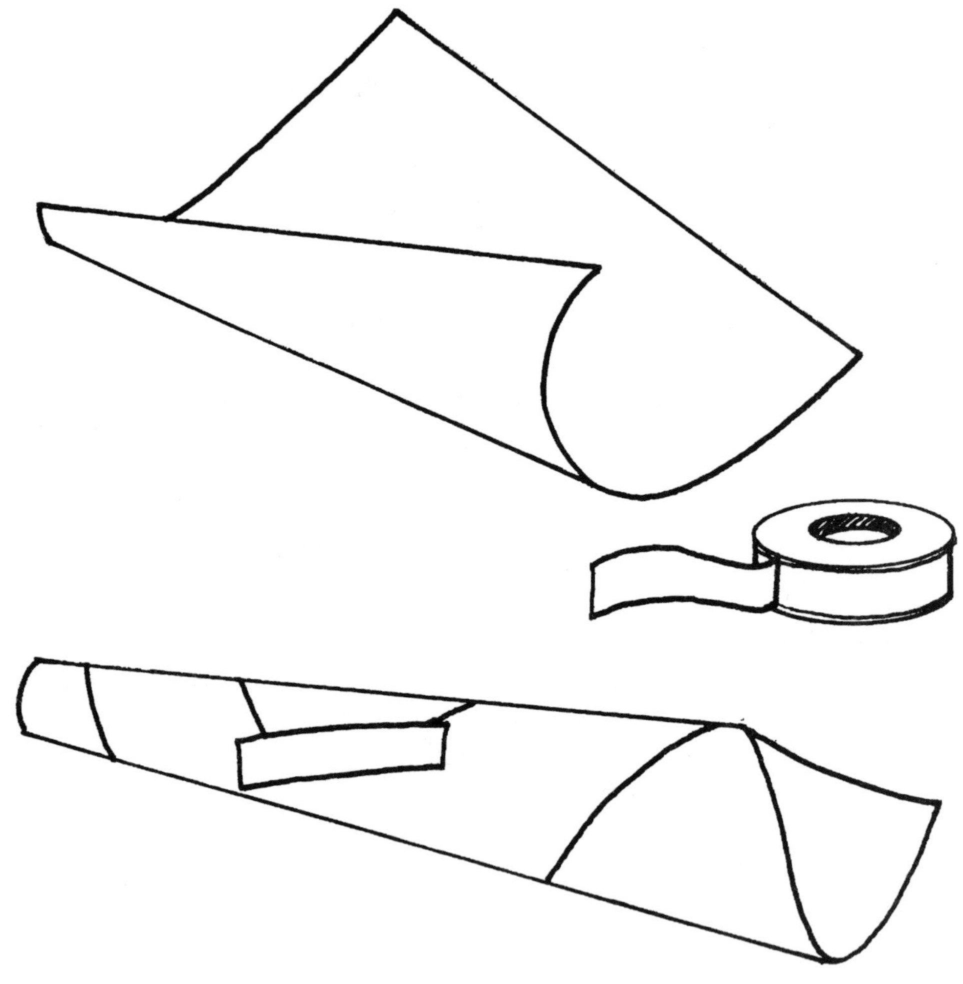

HOME CONNECTION

Children can teach their parents how to make a megaphone at home. Parents can use it to call the children in from outdoors.

Purpose: This activity shows children that sound can be magnified and directed by a megaphone.

Materials: file folders or thick colored paper
tape

Preparation:

1. Lay a file folder flat, cut it in half, and starting at one corner, roll the sheet into a cone. If file folders are not available, use thick colored paper.

2. The small end should be at least approximately 2.5 cm. wide.

3. Tape the cone shape in place. For hygienic purposes, each child should have his own megaphone with his name on it.

4. Show the children how to hold the megaphone close to their lips and speak into it. Make different length megaphones and notice that the longer the cone, the more the voice tone will change by vibration.

Activity: Use the megaphone outdoors so that the children can be as loud as they like. Let the children move freely around the yard and have them take turns calling out a message to the group: "All children go to the sand box." "All children come for a ticket (have small pieces of paper for tickets)." "Everybody meet at the door."

A megaphone is a versatile prop when children are involved in dramatic play. For example, they can pretend to be firefighters calling people in high buildings, a lifeguard supervising at the beach or pool, the captain of a ship calling to another ship when his radio fails, or a teacher calling children together at a park.

Extensions and variations:

- Children can experiment with singing through their megaphones either as a group or individually.

 to 

The Money Box

Submitted by Step by Step Slovakia

HOME CONNECTION

Call parents' attention to the fact that there is great potential for pretend play in many ordinary household objects. They can encourage their children's creativity by pointing out simple objects (for example, a pot or a wooden spoon) and asking, "What could this be?"

Purpose: Dramatic play develops the creativity, imagination, and social skills of young children. A rich dramatic play environment frees children to express themselves and experiment with both real and fantasy situations. The money box is a prop that can be used by children in a number of different play scenarios, including a store, a post office, or a bank. As children use the money box to dramatize their experiences, they will discover their own uses for it.

Materials:

yogurt cups	tape
colored paper	glue
crayons	scissors

Preparation:

1. Measure and cut paper to fit around a yogurt cup. Let the children draw a picture or design on the paper according to their personal preferences. They can glue the paper in place so it covers the cup.

2. On paper, trace around the circular opening of the yogurt cup. Cut the paper circle and a slit that will accommodate coins or pretend money. Secure this opening on top of the yogurt cup with glue or tape.

Activity: A money box can be casually introduced to a group of children as they are engaged in play. This is most easily done as the teacher enters into the play situation with a comment such as, "You may want to use this money box to hold your make-believe money."

Extensions and variations:

- Place some real coins for the older children in the money box. Ask the children to name them. How much is each coin worth? Are some coins of equal value? Which are worth the most, the least?

LITERACY

 to 

Touch-and-Tell Mystery Box

HOME CONNECTION

Encourage parents to use descriptive language when they speak with their child. Encourage patience, as young ones ask constant questions. Although at times children's search for information can be bothersome, adults must remember that children are in fact looking for information about the world. Their questions let us know their interests and focus from moment to moment. Help parents appreciate this fact when you share this activity with them by sending home a short note.

Purpose: Children use the sense of touch to explore and evaluate experience. The touch-and-tell mystery box is an instructive addition to the literacy area because children expand their vocabularies as they describe what they feel. This mystery box activity involves nature items, but the variety of objects that can be contained in the box is endless. This experience focuses on the children's ability to feel, observe, and communicate their observations. They discuss number, texture, shape, and size. They develop the ability to discriminate tactilely between various items.

Materials: medium-sized box
collection of rocks, acorns, branches, leaves, shells, feathers

Preparation:

1. Cut a hand-sized hole in a medium-sized box.

2. Collect 2 specimens of a variety of items: rocks, feathers, acorns, tree branches, leaves, shells, etc.

Activity: Put 1 item into the mystery box. Place between 2 and 5 items on the table in the sight of the child. One item must be the same as the item that is in the mystery box. Ask a child to put his hand inside the box and guess which of the items on the table is also in the box. Encourage the child to look at that item on the table and use texture words to describe the item in the box.

Extensions and variations:

- Rather than placing 1 set of items within view of the child, place 2 - 5 items in the mystery box. Then place 1 object from the other set in front of the box. Ask the child to search the mystery box for the same object.

- In a small group of 2 or 3 children, each child reaches into the box and describes 1 of the items. In teaching descriptive attributes, a teacher may ask the child if the item is hard or soft, rough or smooth, cold or warm. The children take turns guessing what the item is, based on the description given. Encourage the use of descriptive language to build vocabulary.

- Teach shapes by placing in a large bag items such as a ball, a square wooden block, and a musical triangle.

- Place 3 pencils of different lengths in a large bag. Ask the child to reach in and remove the shortest pencil. Replace the pencil and ask for the longest pencil. Replace the pencil and ask for the "middle-sized" pencil.

Color Flip Book

 to 

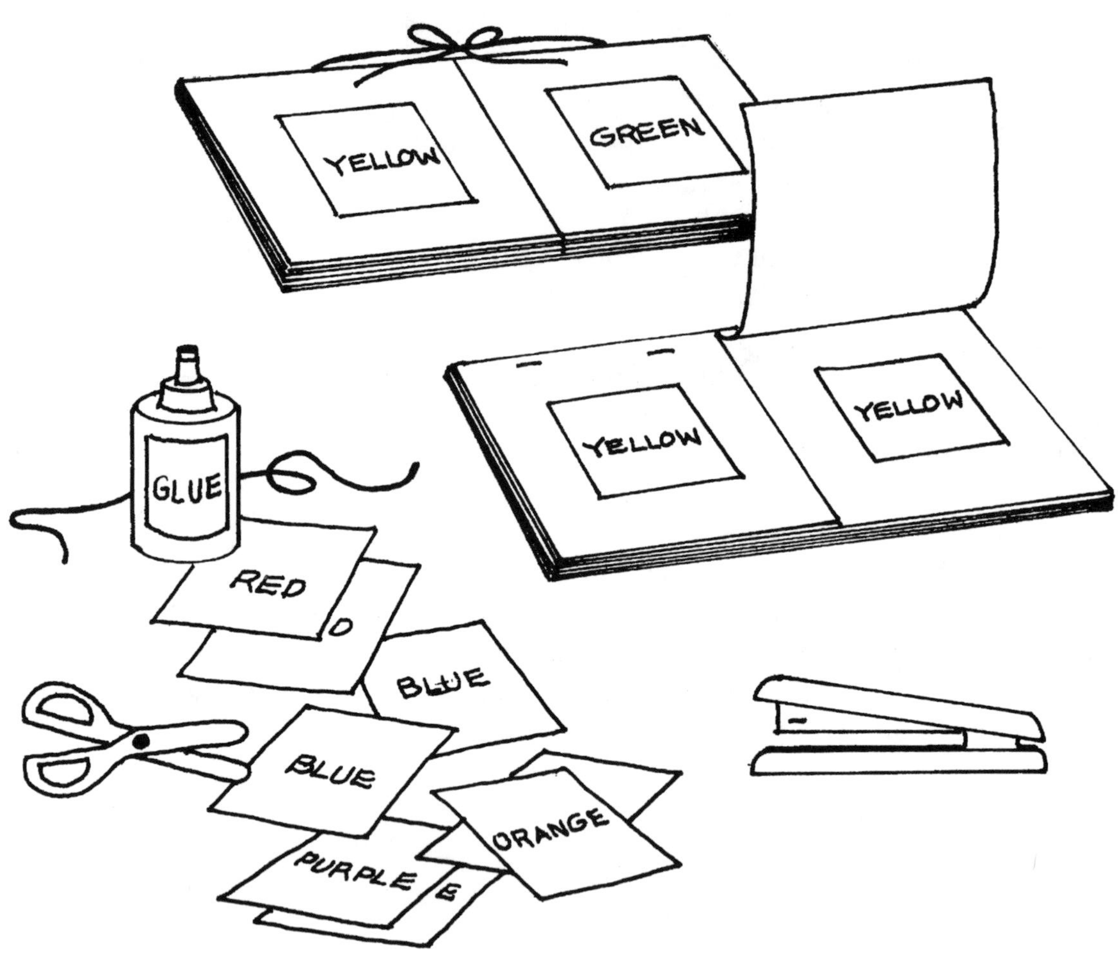

HOME CONNECTION

This simple activity can be adapted at home by parents and children. It is a book for matching colors or pictures that are the same. Parents can start with a child's interest in dogs, for example, and make a flip book with matching pictures of different kinds of dogs.

Purpose: A color flip book is composed of solid color pages. It helps children match or identify colors. The content of a flip book can be changed or added to; the teacher can start with primary and secondary colors for young children and add pastels for older ones.

Materials:

- colored paper
- scissors
- glue
- stapler or string
- string

Preparation:

1. Fold 4 or 5 sheets of colored paper in half. This will give you an 8- or 10-page book.
2. Staple or tie the papers together.
3. Cut up the center with a scissors. Do not cut the bottom page.
4. Cut out the colored squares and glue them on the paper. Use 2 squares of each color, but not opposite one another.
5. Children can now "flip" to mix and match.

Activity: The book can be used in several ways. Give children time to just flip through all the pages. Beginning with the first color on the left side, ask the child, "Can you flip to the same color on the other side?" After the child has done that, move to the second color on the left-hand side. Again ask the child to flip to the same color. Once the child has grasped the idea, you can ask other kinds of questions, for example, "Can you find your favorite color on both sides?"

Extensions and variations:

- Flip books lend themselves to multiple uses. For 5 and 6 year olds make one that matches simple words. A mathematics flip book could match numerals and quantities of objects. Enlist the help of an artistic parent to make matching flowers, leaves, and trees.

Lotto Boards

 to 

Purpose: Lotto boards are boards with pictures or numerals affixed; they are the basis for a variety of matching games. They come in a variety of types, yet they all require observation, comparison of likenesses, and recognition of differences. These matching skills are paramount in learning science, math, and reading readiness concepts. Lotto boards can involve identification of colors, numerals, fruits, and pictures of people and can be created to supplement social studies themes. For example, if types of foods are being studied, a teacher can create fruit, vegetable, and protein lotto boards. By asking open-ended questions, the teacher helps the children to expand their vocabularies.

Materials:

- large piece of cardboard or thick paper
- pencil or marker
- large envelope or file folder
- drawings or pictures from magazines
- cards
- glue
- scissors

HOME CONNECTION

Simple matching activities can be done at home as parents help their child get ready for the day, prepare meals together, and do the marketing. Parents must learn to appreciate the learning involved in such seemingly simple activities and provide time to consider daily activities from the child's point of view.

Preparation:

1. Using a pencil or marker, divide the cardboard into equal sections. The board could have from 9 to 20 sections. Make sure the sections are large enough to hold the pictures being glued onto the board.

2. Make matching cards to correspond to the pictures on the boards.

3. Store each lotto board and its matching pieces in a large envelope or file folder and place in the manipulative area.

Activity: As an individual activity: Place 2 large clips on each matching card for the lotto board. Mix up the pieces. Ask the child to use a magnet to pick up one piece at a time and place it on the corresponding board picture. For a more advanced activity, give the child two lotto boards and 2 sets of cards.

As an activity for 2 children: Using 2 boards, the children take turns. First, one is the caller and the other receives and matches the corresponding card. Then they switch to the second board and the first receiver becomes a caller and the other the receiver/matcher.

Extensions and variations:

- As a small group activity: Prepare many lotto boards with matching drawings or pictures of colors, shapes, names, dots, numerals, fruits, vegetables, people, etc. Give each child a different board and their own set of matching cards. Select a caller.

- As a multicultural activity: Prepare a board with pictures from diverse countries.

- Make texture lotto boards out of a variety of fabric scraps. This activity is particularly good to increase tactile awareness for children with low vision. Ask children to describe the textures—slippery, soft, bumpy—as they play. Make lotto boards by gluing fabric swatches to heavy cardboard. Outline each texture with sticks or straws and secure with glue or tape.

Puppets

Submitted by Step by Step Croatia and Slovenia

Purpose: Puppets are used for many dramatic play experiences. Whether acting out a scene from a story, reliving a life situation, or role-playing a dream, children use puppets to say out loud the things that are on their minds. Puppets stimulate a child's natural use of language. Beside the numerous language, social, and emotional benefits of using puppets in dramatic play, making puppets lets children express their creativity and imaginations. Using a variety of puppets (stick puppets, finger puppets, and bag puppets) allows for choice, encourages new situations, and adds interest.

HOME CONNECTION

Request volunteers to come into the classroom to assist children who may need help. Ask some parents to work together to build a puppet theater for the classroom. This can become an extension of the dramatic play area.

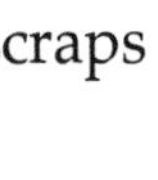

Materials:

sticks, large twigs, or tongue depressors
decorations - yarn, string, buttons
scissors
small paper bags
fabric scraps, paper scraps
glue
newspaper or cotton

Preparation:

1. A younger child can put a bag over the stick and stuff the bag with newspaper or cotton.

2. The teacher helps tie the top of the bag to the stick, making a head.

3. The child can paint or glue decorations onto the head or face.

4. The child dresses the puppet by selecting scraps of paper or fabric.

5. Older children enjoy painting story characters onto durable paper. After they cut out their characters, they glue them onto cardboard and attach them to wooden sticks.

Activity: Some children are reluctant to talk at group times or story times. Almost magically, when these children are holding puppets, they will pretend that the puppet is doing the talking, and they become part of the dialogue. Here are some examples of teacher questions and comments to facilitate language: "This baby will not sleep without a story. Can your puppet tell the baby a story?" "Which does your puppet like best for dessert—fruit, ice cream, or cake?"

Extensions and variations:

- With older children, create a stage set (a large cardboard box works well) or back drop (with a flat sheet). The children paint the scene for puppet play. In Slovenia, children worked together to paint a house for puppet play.

The Important Box

 to 

NAME	DATE	OBJECT

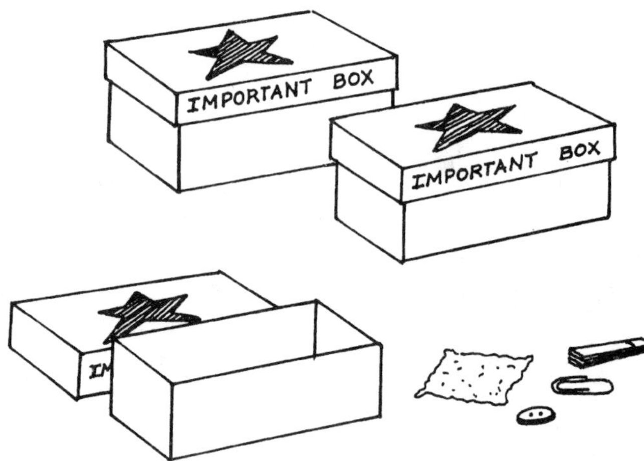

HOME CONNECTION

Meet with the parents of the class. Explain that you are beginning a project to give each child a turn to talk to the class at meeting time. Show the boxes to the parents. Every day, three children will take home a box. Each parent will have two responsibilities:

1. Help the child choose a simple, yet important item that fits into the box—for example, a clothespin, a button, a piece of fabric.

2. Talk with the child about why this item is important. For example, a clothespin lets you hang clothes outdoors to dry. At home, let the child practice how to explain to the class the importance of the item.

Purpose: This activity encourages the development of children's ability to reason and think critically. Children choose and discuss an object that is important to them. The activity expands skills of expressive language that are fundamental to literacy development.

Materials: 3 boxes of the same size
paper
marker

Preparation:

1. Label each box "THE IMPORTANT BOX."

2. Prepare a chart with the names of the children in the class.

Activity: Meet with the children and explain that the class is starting a project about things that are important to each person in the class. Show them the boxes. Tell them that they will each have a turn to take a box home and choose something that is important to put in the box. They should think about why the object is important and be ready to tell everyone in a loud clear voice. Let the children know that you have explained the activity to their parents, who will help them get ready when it is their turn.

As the activity progresses, keep a chart on the wall that lists what each child brought.

Extensions and variations:

- After each child has had a turn, write a simple report listing the objects brought in by the children to be sent home to parents.

- Place the objects in a bag and have the children take turns trying to find their item using only the sense of touch.

A Book about Me

 to 

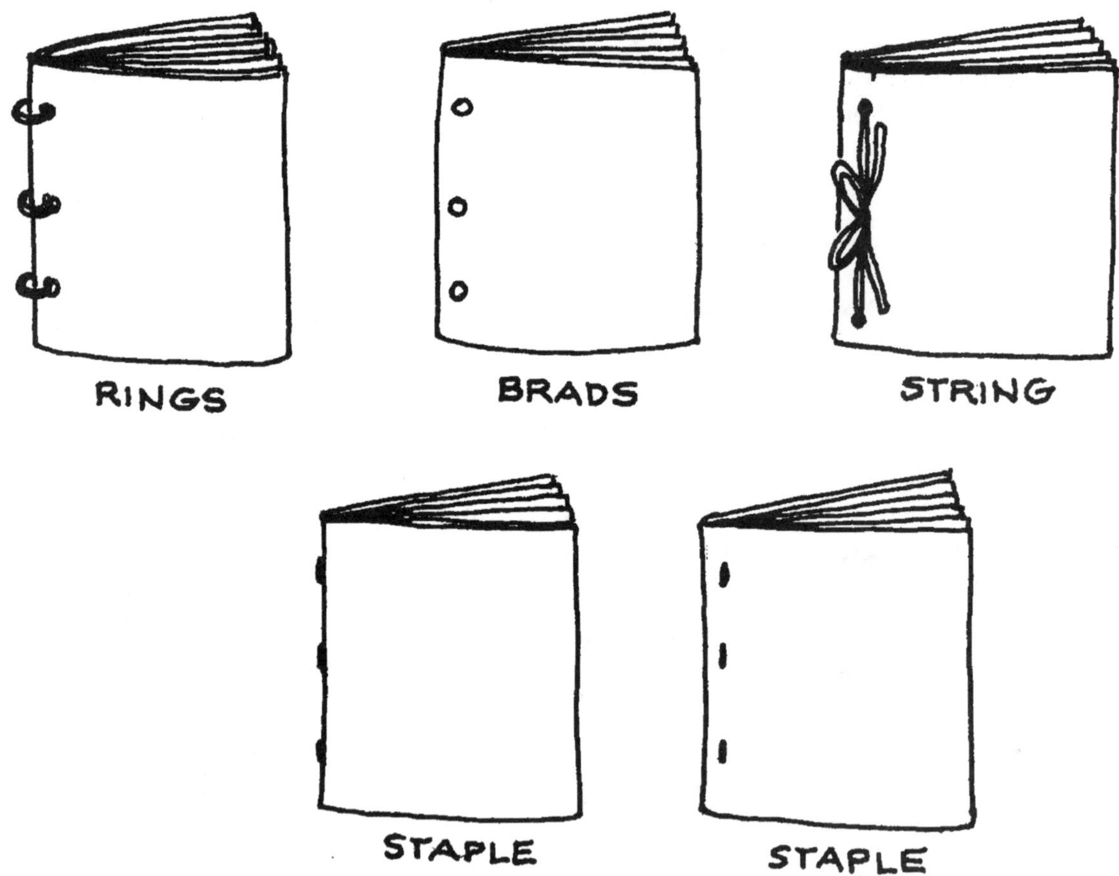

HOME CONNECTION

Announce that you are having a book-making meeting for parents, at which the parents will make blank books for children to use to create their own stories. (See the list of materials that parents will need to make the books.) If possible, have refreshments available to make this an opportunity for people to get to know one another and build spirit.

Purpose: Literature gives children new insights and understanding. It stimulates thinking and language development. To encourage a love of books, read to children every day and plan opportunities for children to make their own books. This activity provides a chance for choices as children select their own topics and build on their own interests. The activity also invites children to think about different ways of assembling books. Making books with children allows teachers to customize content for any teaching domain. "A Book about Me" fits with the study of personal growth as children look back to their younger years. In this way, a child begins to appreciate changes in nature and growth over time.

Materials:

- thick colored paper
- scissors
- stapler
- rubber bands
- cardboard
- cord or yarn
- glue
- hole puncher
- paper fasteners
- old magazines, catalogs, greeting cards, etc.

Preparation:

1. This activity takes place over several months. After the parents have prepared the blank books, children work in small groups or individually to fill the pages in their books. The teacher should take a photo of each child for the book cover and paste it on to cardboard.

2. As the children learn about color, seasons, measurement, senses, and physical growth, they add new drawings, pictures, and words to their books.

Activity: During circle time or morning meeting, explain to the children that they will be making "A Book about Me." Each book will be a little different because each person is unique, but all people are alike in many ways too. "What are some ways we are all alike?" Over time, some of the activities that might be included in the book are my hand prints, footprints, fingerprints; how many members in my family; color of my eyes; my favorite color; a story about me when I was a baby; my favorite thing to do. The children can dictate to the teacher and draw pictures to accompany the narrative.

When the books are completed, the teacher should place them in the literacy area for the children to look at. They will love seeing themselves and other children. The activity helps children build a positive approach to differences as they gain greater awareness and understanding of their own characteristics and those of their classmates.

GLUE

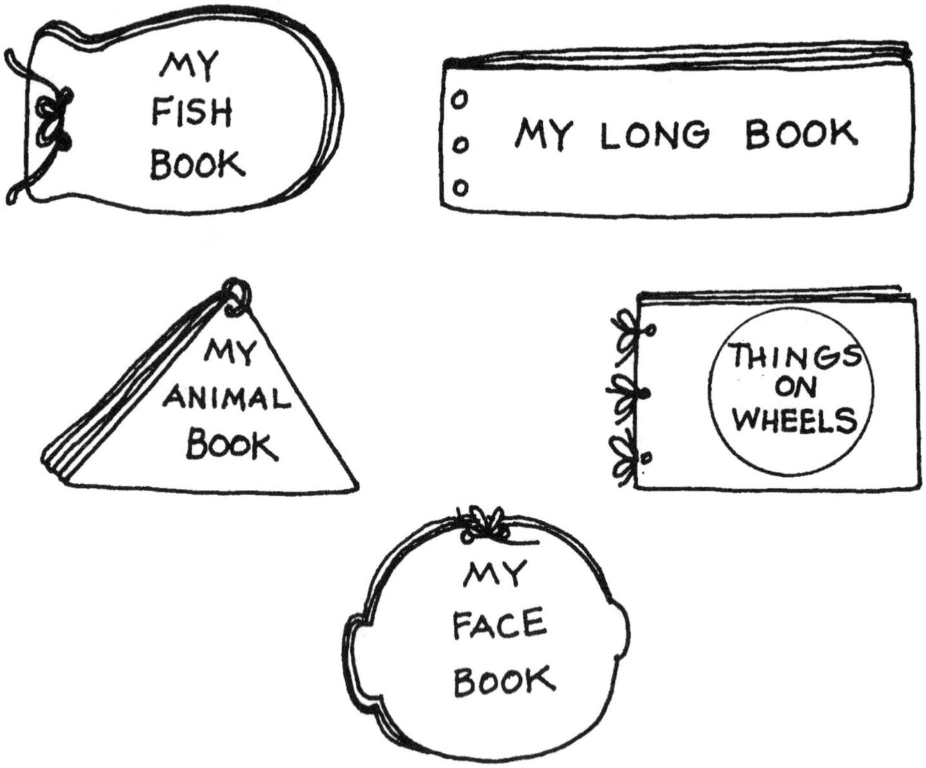

MY FISH BOOK

MY LONG BOOK

MY ANIMAL BOOK

THINGS ON WHEELS

MY FACE BOOK

Extensions and variations:

- Prepare several samples of different shape books. Children choose the shape and topic for the books. Some suggestions may be helpful: people, numbers, cars, airplanes, animals, fruits, vegetables, faces, pets, etc. Make a front and back cover for the younger children and fill it with several blank pages.

- Older children may, with help, select and cut their own shapes and choose their own titles and topics. They cut and paste selected pictures on the blank pages. Younger children may want to dictate stories for adults to write.

- Give the children a choice of different ways to fasten the pages of their book. For example, they may choose to staple or sew their books together with yarn or thread.

- Have children make a book of numbers that are important to them. These can include their ages, house or apartment numbers, number and ages of people in their families, favorite numbers, birthdays, etc.

The Big Catch

Submitted by Step by Step Russia

HOME CONNECTION

Children learn pre-reading skills first by listening to spoken stories. At bedtime retell or read verses to your children that you learned when you were young. Tell them childhood stories about you and your family.

Purpose: This literacy activity is an illustrated child's rhyme that contains a simple math problem to solve by counting, adding, or subtracting. The picture and verse help the children to learn both by sight and by sound.

Materials:	paper	black marker
	paints, chalk, or crayons	tape

Preparation:

1. Select a short, simple rhyming verse and write it in bold, clear lettering.
2. Draw a picture of the action that takes place in the verse, clearly illustrating the math problem that the children must solve.
3. Attach the picture and story together by taping them to heavy paper.

Activity: Although the charm of the Russian rhyme is lost in this literal translation, the simple mathematical elements are apparent in the following verse:

> Two fisherman were sitting on bank.
> Grandpa Korny caught three perch.
> Grandpa Yersey caught a carp.
> How many fish did the fishermen pull out of the river?

During the morning meeting, the teacher reads the verse to the children once or twice. She points to the words as she reads them and asks, "What is happening in the picture?" Together they count the fish. "How many fish did Grandpa Korny catch? How many fish did Grandpa Yersey catch?" Repeat the verse frequently during clean-up time or while walking outdoors.

Leave the picture and verse in the literacy center. The children will return to it, retell the poem, and make up other problems.

Extensions and variations:

- Use verses that relate to classroom themes: boats, fish, astronauts, etc.

Letter Cards

 to 

HOME CONNECTION

Parents should read to their child each day to support growth in literacy skills and language development. Reading together regularly—even if only for a short time—can become an anchor of stability for a young child in a busy day. Send home a note requesting that parents save cartons for use with this activity, which builds pre-reading skills.

Purpose: Distinguishing likenesses and differences is a skill necessary in the development of literacy. In early childhood, children become familiar with letters and how letters form the printed word. They then learn to sort like alphabet letters. In this activity, children build pre-reading skills by matching, sorting, and comparing letter forms.

Materials:

milk cartons
thick colored paper
cards (5 for each letter)
clear contact paper (if available)
scissors
glue
markers

Preparation:

1. Collect as many milk cartons as letters in the alphabet.
2. Trim the cartons and cover them with thick colored paper, then with clear contact paper (if available). Attach 1 letter card to the front of each carton.
3. Make four more cards of each letter of the alphabet.

Activity: Ask the child to sort the letters into the cartons with the matching letters. "Can you name the letters?" Some 5 year olds can begin making sound-symbol associations.

Extensions and variations:

- Similar sorting cartons can be made for colors, shapes, and numbers.
- To develop sight words, attach cards with short (2- and 3-letter) words to the sorting cartons. Make the corresponding cards to go in the cartons.
- As children learn the sounds of each letter, they can select cards with pictures of objects that begin with the same initial sound, such as "S" for snake, sun, stick, soap.

ART

Seed Collage

 to 

Submitted by Step by Step Romania

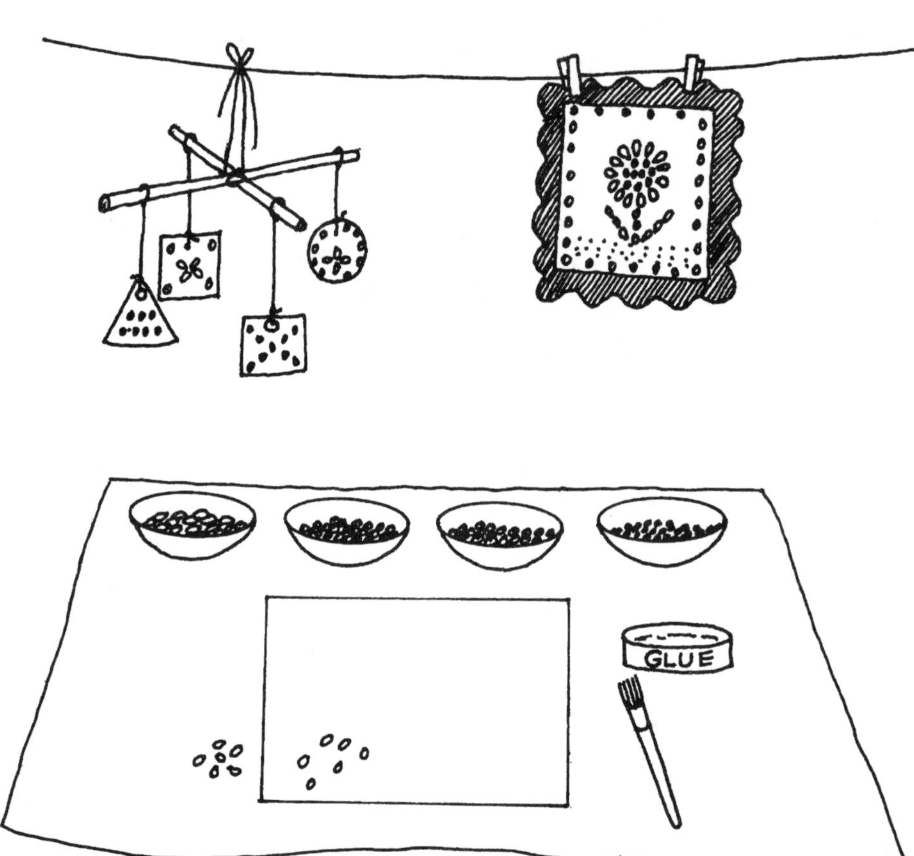

Purpose: Children delight in touching things and exploring textures and sizes. Using seeds as part of a collage offers children a tactile way to experience 2-dimensional surfaces. Sensory exploration is essential for physical and cognitive development in young children. While making a seed collage, children can discuss nature and how plants grow. Seeds can also be used to sort, categorize, and count. Making a collage, the children learn vocabulary words such as *small, big, soft, smooth, rough, bumpy, scratchy*, etc.

HOME CONNECTION

Remind parents that tactile exploration is an important way that children learn. Parents should encourage children to touch and feel materials used in cooking, gardening, and household chores. A parent and child can make a collage together using seeds or other material available from home.

Materials: water in small jar or plastic cup
separate containers (bowls) for seeds
a variety of seeds - watermelon, pumpkin, sunflowers, squash
white glue
paint brush
newspapers
thick paper

Preparation:

1. Cover a table or floor with newspaper.
2. Put watermelon, pumpkin, sunflower, and squash seeds into separate bowls.
3. Dilute white glue with water in a small jar or plastic cup.
4. Give each child a piece of thick paper and a paint brush.

Activity: The children paint the glue onto the paper where they want the seeds to be glued. Young children should be guided in this process. Talk with children about selecting the seeds they want for their collages. They choose which seeds to use and where to place them. Talk about how the picture will feel and look as they choose the seeds. They can sprinkle the seeds like rain falling onto the glued area. Allow the glue to dry. Lift paper, shake off the loose seeds, and return them to the bowls.

Extensions and variations:

- A teacher may select a theme for the collages, such as shapes, birds, or faces.
- A group of children can work together on one large collage.
- Seeds may be sorted by attributes for a mathematics activity. Begin by placing all the seeds in one container. Ask the children to put like seeds in piles. Later, ask them how they decided to group the seeds. Play a guessing game to see if someone can guess how a group was sorted—for example, by color or size.
- After the children have finished their collages, place the remaining seeds in one container. Ask the children to estimate how many seeds are in the container and then count them.
- Older children may want to make several seed collages, cut out them out, and string them together to make a mobile.
- Older children may sketch out a design or picture, place the seeds in their pictures, and then paint the background design or picture with watercolors.

 to 

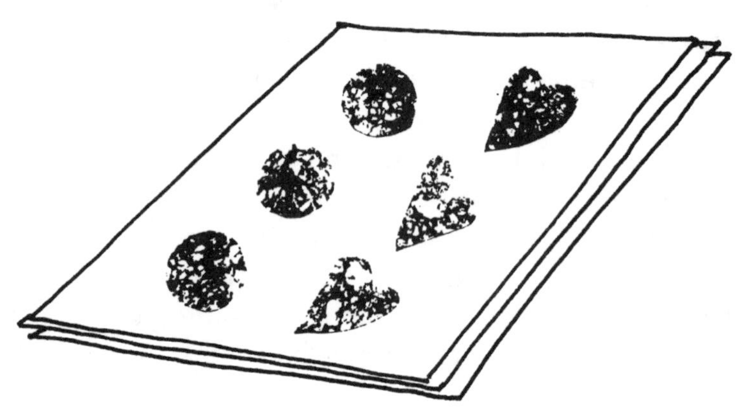

HOME CONNECTION

Parents and children can work on this activity together to make personalized wrapping paper for birthdays and holidays.

Purpose: This activity gives children the experience of transferring images from a 3-dimensional object to a 2-dimensional surface. Printmaking is a method of creating an image by transferring the surface of an object to a piece of paper or another surface.

Printmaking can promote problem-solving and critical-thinking skills. As each child selects from among a collection of objects, she has to decide where to imprint the image on paper, how many objects to use, and how often to imprint each one. Printmaking also develops fine-motor and visual discrimination skills. The idea of gathering objects found at home or in nature illustrates a resourcefulness necessary in daily life.

Materials:

newspapers
white or colored paper
sponge or folded paper towels on a tray
tempera paint - several colors

collection of three-dimensional objects such as: bottle caps, small wooden scraps, box tops, seashells, spools, nuts and bolts, cookie cutters, erasers, small sponges cut into shapes, etc.

Preparation:

1. Soak a moistened sponge or folded paper towel with tempera paint.

2. Press the selected object into the sponge or paper towel.

3. Stamp the object onto the paper.

4. Repeat the process using the same or different objects, as many times as desired.

Activity: The designs of younger children are not likely to resemble a pattern. As they mature and have more printmaking opportunities, patterns may emerge. Young children need time to explore and discover, without teachers suggesting what they should do.

With older children, help them discover that repeating shapes and colors make a pattern. Teachers can show designs in fabrics, wallpaper, and other decorative materials to children. Use open-ended questions to encourage the children to explore the idea of patterns: "Where have you seen patterns?"

Extensions and variations:

- Use sponge shapes (stars, triangles, diamonds, circles, etc.) for printing objects. The sponge shapes should be cut by a teacher using scissors.

- Take children on a nature walk and collect items from the environment for printing.

Finger Painting

 to 

HOME CONNECTION

Emphasize to parents that young children learn by doing. Children should not be inhibited by worries that they will get dirty at school. Let parents know that smocks will be provided for painting activities. Parents should send children dressed in play clothes, ready for play and exploration!

Purpose: Finger painting is a familiar early childhood activity. It encourages the child's sense of touch and discovery of how colors change or form new colors when mixed together. When done collectively, finger painting also encourages social interaction as children paint and discover together.

Materials: masking tape, finger paint: blue, yellow, red, smocks

Preparation:

1. Select a table with a clean washable surface area for painting and 2 jars of finger paint (use primary colors).

2. Place masking tape on the surface of the table to separate the space into 4 equal sections. Assign 2 children to one side of the table and give them the same color of paint. Assign the other 2 children to the other side of the table; give them the other color paint. Let them paint by themselves.

3. Remove the masking tape and allow the children to paint more freely, without regard to space restrictions. As they begin to work jointly, children will see how colors change as they are mixed together. They will also communicate with each other as they share their sense of excitement about the finger painting activity.

Activity: Tell the children that they are conducting a science experiment. Explain that for a short time they must finger paint in their own sections, defined by the tape. Show each child her section and her paint. If children ask for the other color, explain that in a little while they will have the other color, but for now each child must use the color in front of her. When you see that the children's interest in finger painting is waning, remove the masking tape and tell the children that they can now paint across the table with their partners. Often, children paint toward one another and begin to talk. As they mix the paints, the colors change and new colors emerge. When the children are finished, the teacher should try to find space on the table to write the names of the children who created the painting. The teacher asks, "What happened to the colors?" She explains that all colors come from mixing the primary colors of red, yellow, and blue.

Extensions and variations:

- Make a "print" of the painting. Take a sheet of newsprint and put it onto the painted surface. Press gently and carefully lift the paper.

- Use different combinations to make new colors.

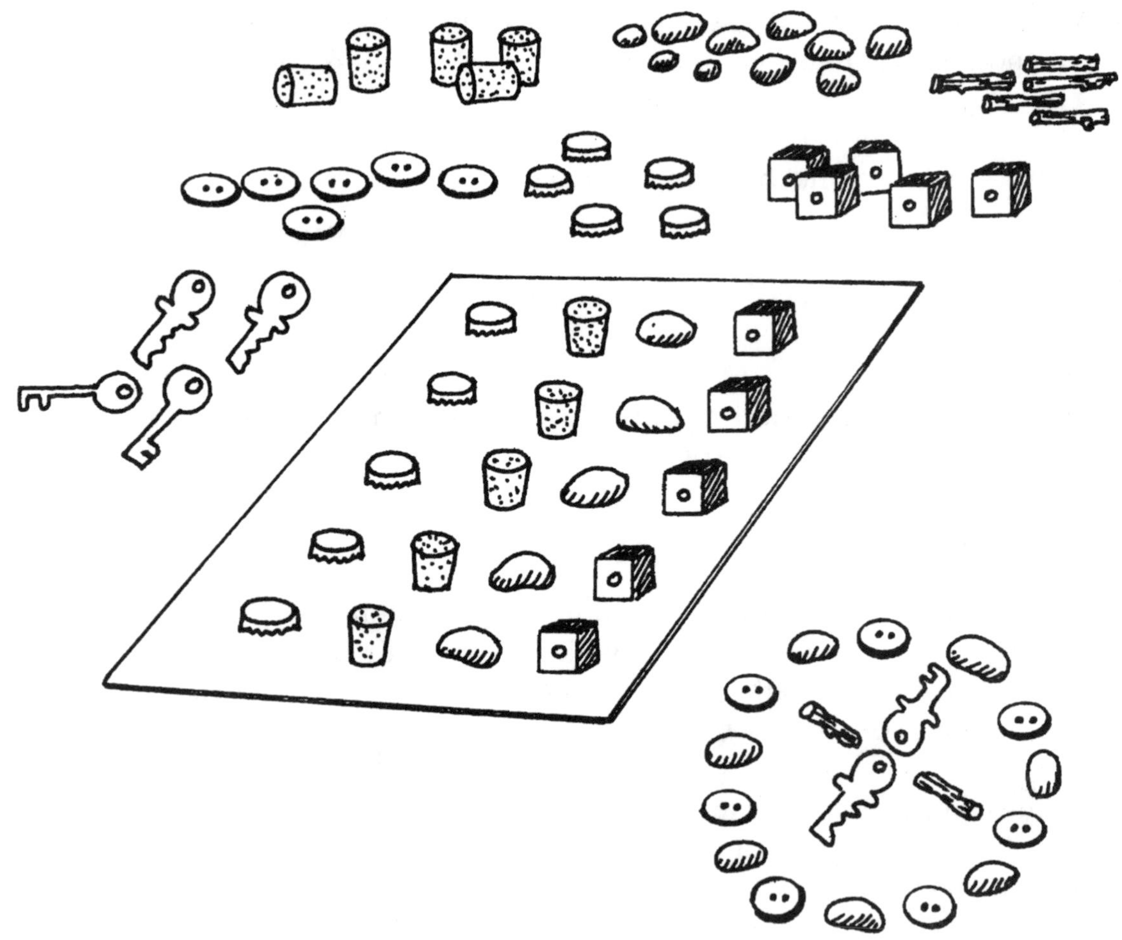

HOME CONNECTION

Send a note home to parents, encouraging them to incorporate pattern recognition into daily activities. Parents and children can make a game of looking for patterns in their homes and outdoors. While walking or riding together, parents and children can invent sound patterns and take turns repeating each other's patterns.

Purpose: Recognizing patterns is a key to mathematical thinking. Number systems are based on sets of patterns. Children need to work with patterns so that they can gain an understanding of concepts in mathematics. These experiences should be in a visual, verbal, and physical format. Looking for patterns is necessary for making generalizations, seeing relationships, and understanding the logic and order of mathematics.

Materials:

- bottle caps
- keys
- buttons
- unit blocks
- stones
- corks
- small sticks
- colored cubes

Preparation:

1. With the child or children watching, lay out a pattern with objects—for example, cork, stone, cork, stone.

Activity: Ask a child to extend the pattern using the objects in the same order. Encourage children to talk about the pattern that they see. Talking about the pattern will get them used to analyzing patterns. Next ask the child to copy the pattern using new materials.

Extensions and variations:

- If a child does not want to explore patterns, suggest that he play as he chooses. He may find a pattern on his own.

- Have the children create patterns with objects, action, and words. Some examples are: snap, clap, snap, clap; hum, sing, sing, hum, sing, sing, hum; stand, sit, kneel, stand, sit, kneel.

- Go on a walk inside or outside the school and look for patterns.

See-Through Strips

 to 

HOME CONNECTION

Since cellophane may be difficult to acquire, ask parents to save cellophane candy wrappers or flower wrappings for this project.

Purpose: Color see-through strips will help children learn how colors combine to make new colors—specifically, how the combination of two primary colors creates a secondary color. The children can relate the colors to familiar objects.

Materials:
scissors
masking tape
red, yellow, and blue cellophane papers or acetate strips

Preparation:

1. Collect red, blue, and yellow cellophane or acetate strips. Cut 2 of each color into 12 cm. x 5 cm. strips.

2. If using acetate strips, cover the sharp edges with masking tape.

Activity: Gather 4 children together. Give each child a color strip. Have them first look through their individual color strips by holding them up to the light. Each child names something that is the color of the strip—for example, blue is the color of water or the sky. Each child should have a turn.

Put children with different color strips into pairs. Each child in the pair looks through the two strips to see what new colors are made. The teacher now gives each pair another strip, making sure that each pair has a set of red, blue, and yellow. Allow children to explore and exchange color strips. When the teacher feels interest is waning, call the children together. Let each pair name the colors produced, and name something that is that color.

Extensions and variations:

- Allow children to cut up pieces of cellophane or acetate and make their own color combinations. They could tape the acetate pieces together to make stained glass windows.

- As an extension of the original activity, the teacher might encourage the expression of emotional and impressionistic responses of the children caused by colors. For example, yellow is the color of sunshine and it makes me feel happy. Blue is the color of the ocean and I like the waves in the ocean. Orange is the color of fire and it makes me feel hot.

Rubbings

 to 

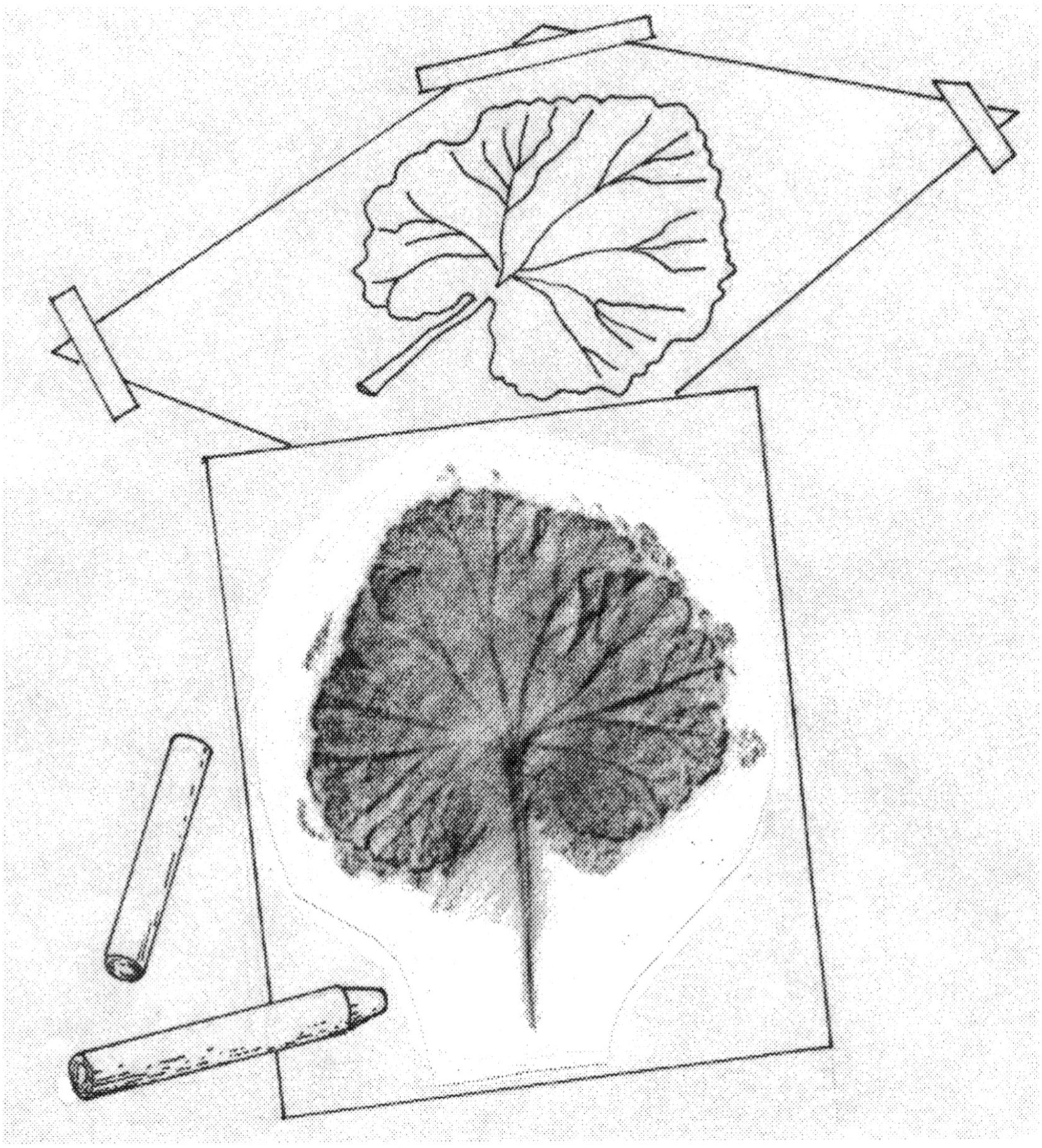

HOME CONNECTION

This activity can easily be adapted to do at home. A child and parent may decide to do a rubbing from an object at home.

Purpose: By making rubbings, a child learns to produce a "picture copy" of a particular object. The process of rubbing develops fine motor coordination and muscle strength because the child must manipulate a crayon and control the paper and crayon. The child also learns about textures.

Materials:

lightweight white paper
chalk, if crayons are not available
crayons (covers removed)
tape

collection of objects with textures that feel bumpy, rough, ragged, coarse, etc.: coins, leaves, keys, combs, tiles, tree bark, lace scraps, shells, etc.

Preparation:

1. Each child chooses an appealing object or two from the classroom collection or collects objects on a walk.

2. Place a sheet of paper over one or many of the objects listed above. For younger children, it may be necessary to tape the corners of the paper to the table.

3. Next, make a rubbing by taking a large crayon or piece of chalk, holding it on its side, and gently rubbing back and forth over the surface of the object. The impression should instantly appear.

Activity: Explain to the children that they will make copies of collected objects and that the copies will be made in a special way. Young children will be excited by what happens when they do the rubbing. For them, the process is more important than the product. Vocabulary words such as *over, under, thickness,* and *flatness* should be emphasized throughout the activity.

Extensions and variations:

- In pairs or small groups, children can complete a rubbing and then ask their friends if they recognize the object.

- Take a "Rubbings Walk" around the classroom or outdoors. Children will need crayons and paper in hand!

- Wash over the rubbings with watercolors. (See *Wax Resist* on page 158)

- For older children, separate rubbings could be put together to create a larger picture. For example, a child could create the face of a person by using the rubbings of coins or buttons for eyes and tree bark for hair! Ask the children to use their imaginations in designing pictures and scenes.

Wax Resist

 to 

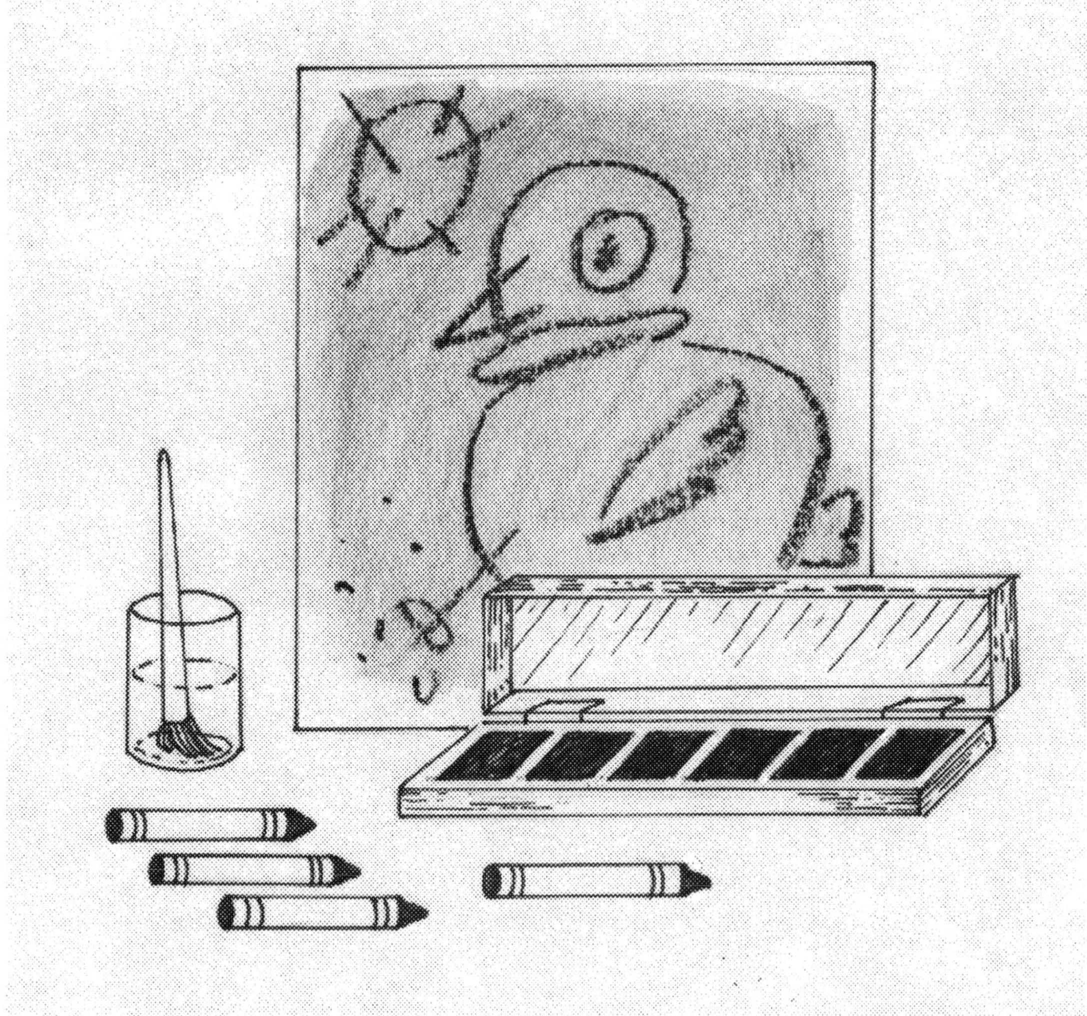

HOME CONNECTION

In a short note to parents, list the steps their children followed to create their wax-resist pictures. Emphasize that parents should value the "art," even if it does not appear polished and realistic. Encourage them to display their children's art work proudly at home.

Purpose: Wax resist is an art technique in which pictures drawn with crayons are washed over with watercolors, thereby creating a "magical" effect. A wax resist is a simple project that is appropriate for younger and older children who enjoy exploring the resist process and experimenting with color, textures, designs, and drawings. This activity promotes small muscle development, decision-making, and planning skills.

Materials:

white paper	container of water
crayons	watercolors
newspapers	paint brushes

Preparation:

1. Put newspapers on the tables or floor where children will work.

2. Give each child a piece of white paper, crayons, and watercolors. Provide a container of water for rinsing paint brushes.

Activity: Ask the children to draw a design or picture on the paper with crayons. Encourage them to press firmly with the crayons. When the drawing is finished, the child paints over the picture with watercolors.

Their creations come to life after the watercolors are applied; the children will call the discovery magic. Clarify by explaining, "Not magic, science! It happens because the wax in the crayons coats the paper and protects it from the water. The wax resists the water."

Extensions and variations:

- Instead of using watercolors, brush black ink, tempera paint, or food coloring over the entire paper.

- Create a different effect by drawing with crayons on black paper and wash over it with diluted white tempera paint.

- Connect the activity with thematic teaching units or favorite storybooks that have been read aloud in class. If the class is learning about leaves, children can use leaves to make wax resists. Or, ask the children to make a wax resist that illustrates their favorite part of a story.

Box Weaving

 to 

Submitted by Step by Step Lithuania

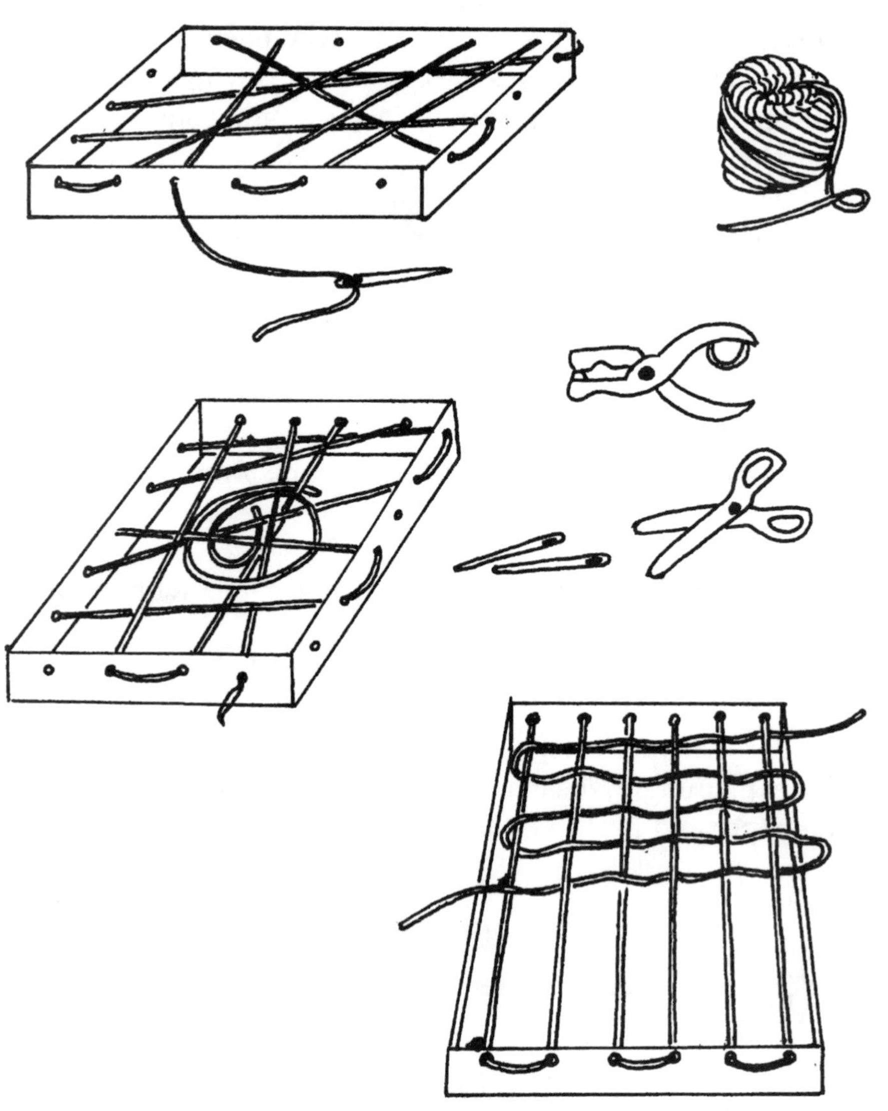

HOME CONNECTION

Often parents and other family members have skills and talents that they will happily share if they are asked. For example, many relatives may welcome the opportunity to come to the classroom and demonstrate weaving techniques. Have a visitor who weaves come and talk to the children about how she first learned to weave. Have the visitor stay and weave while the children work.

Purpose: Weaving teaches children patterns and the basic principle of how fabric is made. It encourages them to use their small motor skills, practice sequential thinking, and understand spatial relationships.

Materials:

- lid of a box (preferably cardboard)
- variety of colorful yarn
- scissors
- hole punch
- plastic needle

Preparation:

1. To prepare the lid for weaving, punch holes around the entire edge of the box lid approximately 1 - 2 cm. apart.

Activity: With 2 or 3 children watching, demonstrate how to put the end of the yarn through a hole and tie it securely (make the knot on the inside of the box lid). Put the yarn through a needle and let the children thread the yarn across the box lid, going back and forth into different holes. Patterns may begin to appear. Demonstrate how a second colored yarn will add more pattern and color to the weavings. A third colored yarn can be added in the middle by doing finger weaving. Let the children make their own patterns.

Extensions and variations:

- As the children become more experienced at handling yarn on a threaded needle, they can be encouraged to move on to the next step. String yarn from top to bottom of box lid. Using a piece of yarn threaded on a needle, the children will weave over and under, over and under, experiencing how real fabric is woven. Start at one end, leaving a tail to tie later. Make sure the yarn is stretched evenly and stays taut and rigid. (Children will need help threading the yarn. They can also do finger weaving using thicker yarn, which is less frustrating for little fingers.)

- For more artistic expression, beads and feathers can be incorporated into the weaving.

- Children like knowing about weaving. Encourage them to examine and think about things that are woven. Also encourage them to think about nature's weavers: spiders and birds.

- In Lithuania, teachers secure a fishing net over a box or wooden frame. Children weave ribbons in and out of the fishing net, creating their own designs as they weave.

Food Carton Mobiles

 to 

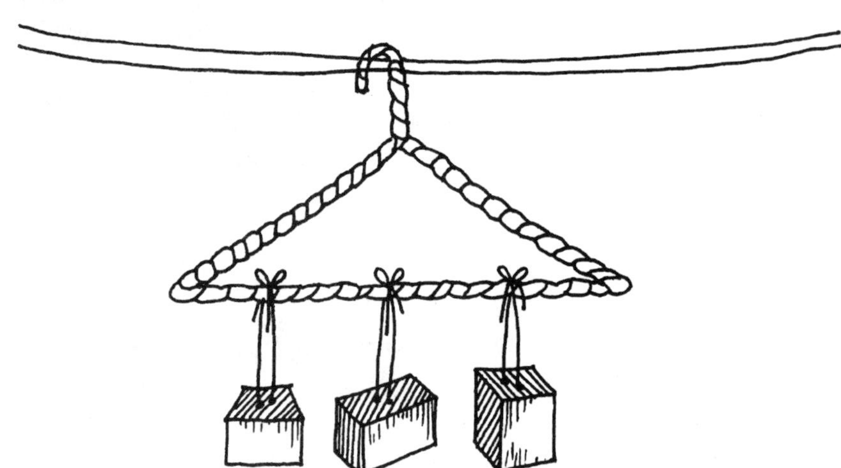

Purpose: These mobiles are "hanging constructions" or 3-dimensional creations assembled from empty food cartons. By creating mobiles, children explore the concepts of balance, gravity, and weight. Early experiences of this kind contribute to mathematical thinking about spatial relationships and equations. As they experiment with color, shape, and design, children express themselves artistically and begin to develop aesthetic appreciation for self-made objects.

Materials:

glue
pencils
string, yarn, or pipe cleaners
scraps of colored construction paper, crepe paper, yarn, or colored tape
scissors
tape
one wire clothes hanger per child
small food cartons or boxes

Preparation:

1. Before involving the children in this activity, wrap the clothes hangers with colored tape, crepe paper, or yarn. Cover all sharp edges to prevent scrapes and cuts.

HOME CONNECTION

Point out to families the usefulness of "throw away" materials. Encourage children and families to collect objects of potential use for art and science activities. A family recycling project for collecting such objects is a worthwhile and enjoyable activity.

2. Ask the children to select some food cartons to hang from the hangers.

3. Tie or tape varying lengths of string, yarn, or pipe cleaners to the cartons.

Activity: Mobiles can be complex or simplified for young children. Offering different materials for attaching the boxes to the hangers is one way of adapting the activity to differing ages. For example, 4 year olds can attach thick pieces of yarn using pre-cut pieces of tape. Parents or other adult helpers can assist younger children to tie the yarn to the hanger.

To begin this activity gather the children and ask if anyone can stand on one foot. Ask for volunteers to demonstrate. Point out that the child is "balancing" her weight on one foot. Distribute pencils (or sticks) and ask the children to try to balance them horizontally across two fingers. Give them a few minutes to try. Next, display a mobile to the group. Point out that the horizontal line of the mobile is balanced by the hanging objects. Tell the children that they are going to make their own mobiles. The children then begin work on their mobiles, tying the cartons to the hangers and experimenting with different placement of the cartons to determine the best positions for balance.

This activity can be done in two parts for older children who may want to spend time decorating their boxes before attaching them to the hanger. Younger children should be focused on the idea of attaching the boxes to achieve a balanced mobile. When the mobiles are complete, ask the children what happens if they move the strings, yarn, or pipe cleaners holding the boxes closer together or farther apart. Have them experiment and make comparisons. Hang the mobiles around the room.

Extensions and variations:

- Create mobiles that relate to a teaching theme, such as an "autumn" mobile.

- Older children can work collaboratively on a larger mobile.

Making an Art Easel

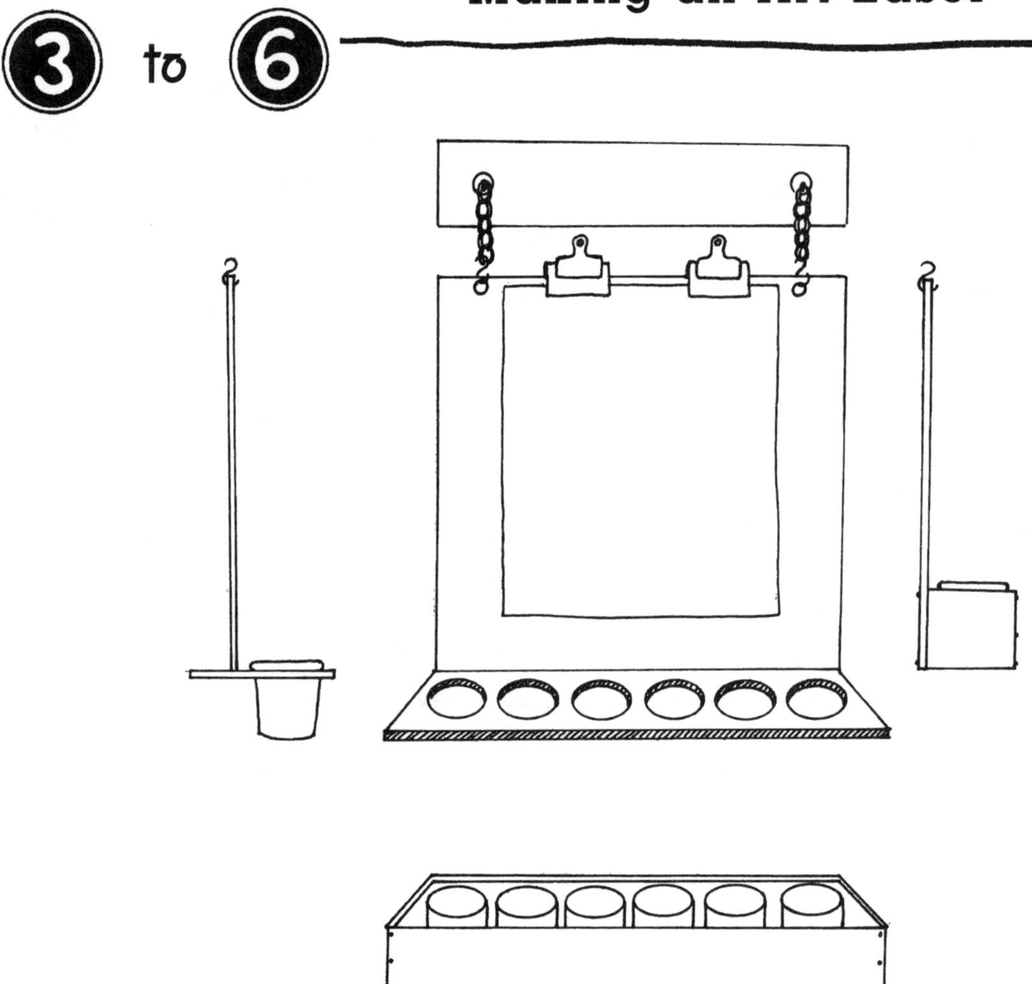

Purpose: An easel is important classroom equipment. The easel described here is portable so that it can be used indoors and outdoors. It can be hung on a wall at an appropriate height or moved outside and hung on a fence. Young children need a space to paint; finding these spaces in a classroom needs to be well thought out. Handy parents can help to make the easel.

Materials:

a wooden board about 60 cm. x 62 cm., weatherized, if possible
2 metal clamps
drill
2 S-shaped hooks
wood (12 cm. x 60 cm.)
nails

Preparation:

1. Cut out easel board.

2. Drill holes in top for hooks.

3. Cut board for paint holder and cut holes to hold paint containers, measuring the hole size carefully. Or, make a paint box to hold paints and nail onto easel board at base.

The diagram shows this easel from the side and front views. It also shows how it can be hung from the wall. The easel with the box can sit on a table because it is designed to stand alone. Use lightweight wood. The easel with tray holes is lightweight and easily moved.

Tips for Painting: When children are painting, a piece of paper or plastic underneath makes clean-up easier. Put tops over paint when not in use.

Activity: Provide children with a selection of colors of paint, paper, and brushes. While 3 and 4 year olds could start out using 2 or 3 colors, as the year progresses they can easily use 5 or 6 colors. The experienced 6 year old painter can select from 6 to 8 colors at a time, or more.

Allow the children to experiment freely with the paint and brushes on paper. Give them as much time as necessary and let them paint more than one picture. With exploration children learn techniques of painting and begin to choose materials and methods appropriate for their creations.

Extensions and variations:

- Set out large chalk pieces for chalk drawings.

- For variety, cut paper into various shapes (round, hearts, etc.) for easel use.

- Use different implements for painting: feathers, cotton swabs, crumpled newspaper, rags, etc.

OUTDOOR
ACTIVITIES

Pressed Leaf Book

Submitted by Step by Step Romania

Purpose: Children learn through direct interaction with tangible objects. The outdoors is a wonderful place to learn and reinforce concepts such as colors, shapes, textures, and sizes. Comparing the characteristics of leaves and making a pressed leaf book furthers the young child's conceptual knowledge base. The children also learn that falling leaves are a characteristic of autumn.

HOME CONNECTION

Encourage parents to spend time looking at the books with their children. They should listen, ask questions, and be receptive to the children's comments.

Materials:

heavy book
glue
white paper
wax paper
brightly colored leaves, including green
metal rings or string

Preparation:

1. Before pressing the leaves in the heavy book, put the leaves in-between wax paper or paper towels to prevent staining the book.

2. Place the leaves between the pages of the book. Find heavy objects to place on top of the book to press the leaves.

3. To make the leaf book, cut pages of equal size and shape and assemble the book (see illustration).

Activity: Take a "leaf walk" and encourage the children to examine the different textures and colors of leaves and then bring them back to the classroom for further handling and examination. Place some of the leaves on display, and ask each child to select a leaf to be pressed and added to a class leaf book.

After the leaves have been pressed, glue them on a page. The teacher can write down the child's words under each leaf: "This is a red, bumpy leaf." "This leaf looks like a star."

Older children can write their names. Children will look at this class book over and over.

Extensions and variations:

- Make leaf rubbings. Place a leaf with its vein-side up under a piece of white paper and rub lightly over the paper with a soft pencil or crayon. Or make leaf prints by pressing a leaf on an ink pad with the vein-side down. Position it on a clean piece of paper. Cover the leaf with another sheet of paper and make the print by gently rubbing with fingertips.

- Flowers can also be pressed and made into a book. Select flowers of varying colors, shapes, and sizes and discuss these attributes with the children.

- Press leaves between sheets of wax paper and iron the paper lightly to seal it. (For safety, be sure an adult helper manages the ironing activity.) Ask the children what caused the wax paper to stick together. Hang the translucent art at the window so that the leaves appear to be falling from the sky.

 to 

Outside Water Painting

HOME CONNECTION

Encourage parents and children to "play paint" together using old brushes and water. This is a time for relaxed, easy interaction; it is a time for parents to listen to their child's comments and observations as the child watches what happens to the water.

Purpose: In this activity, children paint with water on a paved surface or playground. They see the water markings evaporate. This activity helps children see the effect of air and sun on water, as the sun heats their water pictures. Besides exposing children to the concept of evaporation, the activity refines fine and gross motor skills, and facilitates imagination and free exploration.

Materials:
- small pails or wide cups
- water in a pitcher
- large, flat paint brushes

Preparation:

1. Give each child a small pail or wide cup half filled with water and a large paint brush. Have extra water in a pitcher for refills.

2. Talk a walk outside on a sunny day and locate a painting area for the children. Sidewalks, the side of a building, playgrounds, or paved surfaces are most appropriate.

Activity: Begin the activity in small groups. Tell the children that they are going to learn about the science of water and air, which at first seems a mystery. The children will paint outside on a walkway with water and carefully watch to see what happens to their paintings. After they have had ample time to explore this phenomenon of disappearing water, lead the group in a discussion about evaporation: "What happened to the creations? When the sun heats the water, we say the water *evaporates*. Can you think of any other situation where water evaporates?" Have the children paint with water in a sunny area and in the shade. "Are there any differences? Do you think a windy day will speed up evaporation or slow it down? What do you predict will happen on a cloudy day?"

Extensions and variations:

- Place a shallow dish of water outside in the sun. Check the dish at the end of the day.

- Extend the discussion on evaporation by thinking about oceans, rivers, lakes, fog, clouds. Does the sun heat the bodies of water? Does that water evaporate?

- What happens when you put your wet clothes on a clothesline? Set up an outdoor laundry project, with water table or a big tub, soap, clothesline, and clothespins. Hang the clothes in the sun to dry.

 to 

Gardeners

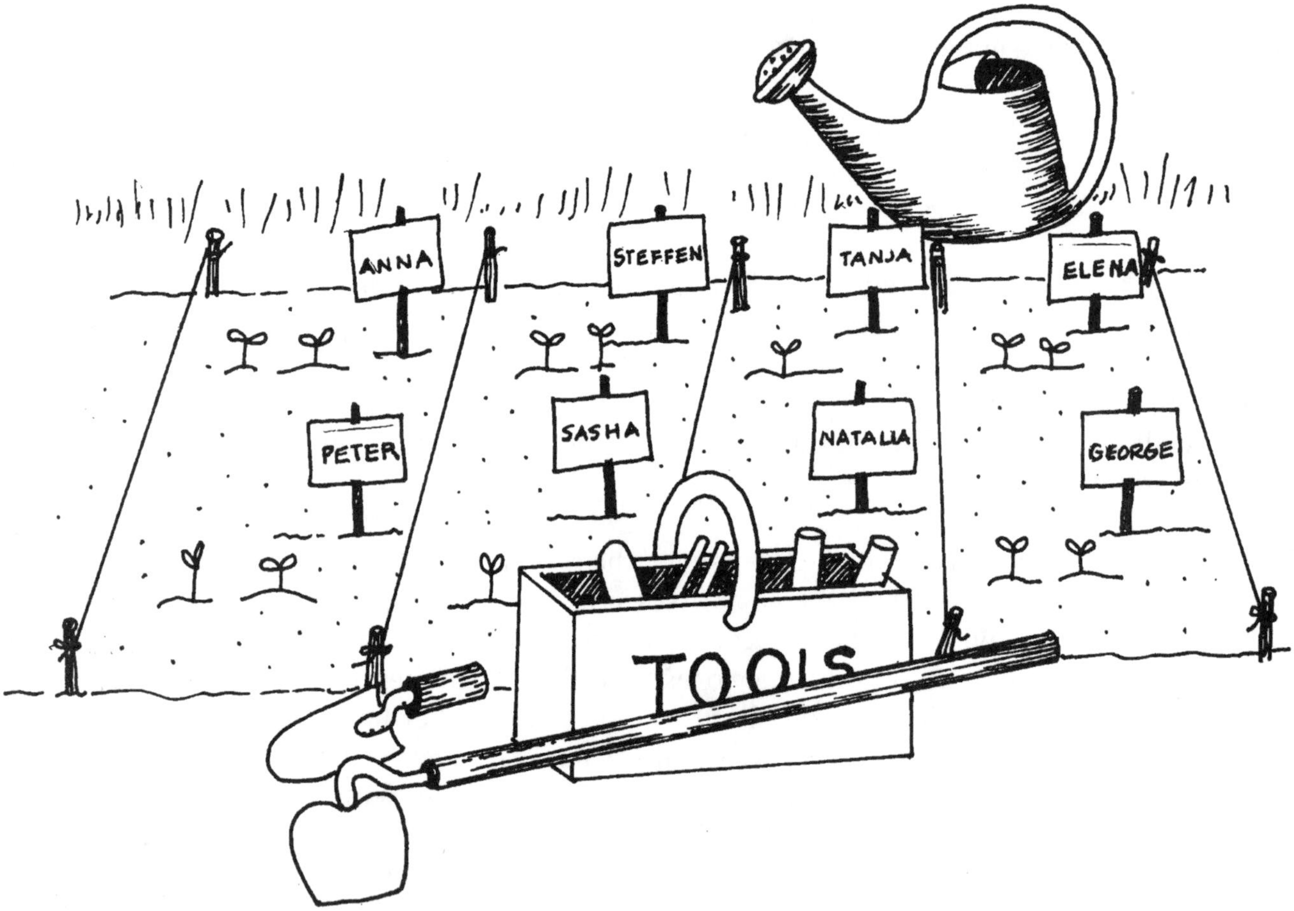

HOME CONNECTION

Parents can plant a seedling or seeds with their child. The child can tend the plant and take responsibility for it.

Purpose: Planting seeds and tending plants is a wonderful learning activity for children of all ages. Gardening can take place either indoors or outdoors. Gardening teaches the elements necessary for growth and sustaining plant life. It also exposes children to concepts such as change, size, shape, and color. Children will learn responsibility and enjoy the rewards of their efforts. They will also learn how seasons affect the garden. They watch the garden during each season and discover the differences.

Materials:

Indoors
- containers for plants
- pebbles
- soil
- large spoons
- water
- seeds or plants

Outdoors
- gardening tools
- seeds or plants
- watering can, hose, or buckets for water
- string and sticks to mark off sections

Preparation:

For indoor planting:

1. Each child should put pebbles in the bottom of a container for drainage and fill the container with damp soil.

2. Plant seeds of herbs (chives, thyme, parsley, or basil), other house plants, or flowers. Cover lightly with soil and pat gently.

3. Water and set the plant containers on a sunny window sill.

For outdoor planting:

1. Find an available outdoor space where children can grow herbs, vegetables, or flowers. Give each child a small space rather than a large one.

2. Have on hand a variety of gardening materials: child-sized garden tools (shovel, rake, hoe, etc.); seeds or plants; access to water (watering cans, hoses, or buckets); string and sticks to mark off the rows or sections.

Activities for indoor gardens: Encourage the children to make their own herb garden containers. Teachers can offer guidance when asked, but let the children make their own decisions about how and what to plant.

Make a few extra plantings. Place a few plants away from the sunlight. Take two different plants and do not give them water. Ask the children if they notice a difference in the growth of the plants in the sun, away from the sun, and without water. Ask, "What do seeds need to grow and live? Do all seeds sprout at the same time?" Help the children notice that the seeds grow in a similar way, but each is a little different. "Can you think of other living things that grow in a similar way, but each of which is a little different?"

Activities for outdoor gardens: A successful garden takes some advance planning. Find a flat place outdoors that has at least 5 hours of sun each day. A 2.5 m. x 2.5 m. area will allow space for several different plants, but a smaller space will do. Add fertilizer or compost to the soil.

Have the children use the gardening tools to plant flowers, vegetables, and herbs. Ongoing maintenance is a must when working in a garden. Encourage cooperative play among small children when weeding, watering, and harvesting. Take time to smell fragrant scents or to admire the brightly colored flowers.

Promote children's thinking by asking questions such as, "Why do you think plants grow toward the light? What do plants need in order to grow?"

Extensions and variations:

- Take children on a field trip to a nursery, greenhouse, farm, or home garden.
- See what lives in the garden soil. Curiosity will be high when earthworms and other soil creatures are found. Look at the soil with a magnifying glass.
- Use graphs to record how long seeds take to sprout. Measure the growth of plants, compare their sizes and shapes.
- Ask a family member who likes to garden to talk to the children about gardening. What is her favorite thing to grow and why? Why does she enjoy gardening? Why is gardening useful to a family?

to

HOME CONNECTION

Parents can provide a shelf or small area at home for children to establish a collection of interesting objects gathered while outside playing or on walks. They should encourage their children to describe the items and tell why they find them interesting.

Purpose: This activity introduces the use of magnification through lenses, a practice important for the study of science. After a nature walk where children touch and observe many natural objects, they will select several items to observe more closely through a magnifying glass. A new word, *magnifying*, will be added to their vocabulary, and they will gain additional knowledge of the importance of "tools of the trade." Along with promoting tactile discrimination, a magnifying glass will encourage curiosity and the development of descriptive language as children talk about natural objects.

Materials:

- cardboard or heavy paper
- magnifying glass
- glue
- natural objects such as nuts and berries

Preparation:

1. Children collect interesting objects from nature, such as pine cones, tree bark, nuts, berries, leaves, rocks, flowers.

2. Glue each object onto a durable piece of paper or cardboard.

Activity: Let the children examine their findings. Then show the children a "magnifying" glass. Notice the rounded shape of the "lens." Discuss respectful care of tools and let the children examine their "specimens." Ask, "What does the magnifying glass do to the items?" Let the children describe what they see.

Some questions to promote discussions are "How does this feel?" "What do you think birds (or animals) do with this?" "Where did we find this?" Encourage children to use descriptive words such as *rough, smooth, texture, slick, bumpy*. Older children should be prompted to expand their descriptions using two or more details, for example, "The rock is round and smooth with lines on it."

Extensions and variations:

- Show the children a pair of magnifying eyeglasses. "What do the glasses do for people?" Look very closely at another child's eye from the side: "Do you see something that looks like a lens? What does it do?"

- The teacher can document the children's descriptions by writing down their words on cards and gluing them next to or under the nature item. This will encourage early literacy skills, and teach children that printed words hold meaning.

 to 

Adopt a Tree

Purpose: This is a year-long project for children. A group of 3 or 4 children "adopts" a special tree that is near the classroom. On regular walks, they observe changes and growth in the tree. They note the differences as the seasons change and see the effects of rain, wind, and other weather conditions. Children compare trees with each other. This science activity encourages children's interest in nature, and helps develop observation and communication skills. It affords an opportunity for teachers to raise questions and thoughts related to the natural world.

Materials:
- several different colors of yarn or string
- crayons or markers
- paper and pencil

Preparation:

1. Once the children have selected a tree that will be their tree to observe, mark each tree with a different color of yarn or string. This helps the children remember and locate which tree they have selected.

2. Make an identification chart showing the location, children's names in the group, and color marker on tree.

HOME CONNECTION

Send a note home explaining this activity to parents. When parents visit the center, suggest that the children take them to see their adopted trees. The children can share their excitement about their trees. Families could also adopt a tree in their neighborhood.

Activity: In autumn, gather the children together in groups of 4 - 5 for a walk around the neighborhood. While walking, the children should pay special attention to the trees. Their group is to choose 1 tree that will be their special tree for the year. After they have chosen the tree, they may draw a picture of it. The small groups should have time to fully explore all aspects of the tree: guess how high it is, how big around the trunk is, how it feels, how it smells, what the leaves look like, etc. Take small groups of children out to observe their trees at different times of the year: with leaves, without leaves, in the snow, in early spring when the first buds appear, when the flowers or seeds appear. If possible, take photos or draw pictures to document the seasonal changes.

Extensions and variations:

- Compare the bark, leaves, and seeds of the trees adopted by the groups. How are they different? Are they alike in any way? With 5 and 6 year olds, call their attention to the leaves. They can be simple or compound, opposite or alternate.

- Encourage the children to give their tree a make-believe name. They may enjoy making up stories about the tree. Some children may want to draw pictures to go with the stories.

- Make leaf prints. The children can collect as many types of leaves as possible. Look for leaves that are not too dry and brittle. Put a little tempera paint on a sponge. Press the leaf against the sponge and then against a piece of paper.

- Make bark and leaf rubbings. Lay a piece of paper against the bark of your tree. Pick up the texture by rubbing the flat side of a crayon over the paper. The same thing can be done in the classroom using leaves.

- Borrow a tree book from the library to help with the identification of your trees. With one child at a time, examine the pictures of trees and notice together similarities and differences in the physical characteristics of the trees. Avoid technical terminology. The older children may enjoy looking through the book to see if they can find a picture of their trees or their classmates' trees.

BLOCKS
MY BRIDGE
A
B
C

Rivers and Bridges

 to 

Purpose: As children build with blocks, they solve problems, use their imaginations, and increase their understanding of size, shape, and space. Block building encourages logical thinking and understanding spatial concepts such as over and under, beside, high and low, wide and narrow, strong and weak. When building together or beside one another, children are learning about teamwork, sharing, and respecting the work of others.

HOME CONNECTION

Parents and children should take walks to see buildings and bridges in their town or city. Children should be encouraged to notice how structures change and to ask questions about how buildings are erected.

Materials:

newspaper
large sheets of paper or paper bags
tempera paint: blue, green, white
pictures of bridges
flat paint brushes
tape
scissors

Preparation:

1. Invite a small group of children to join in creating a make-believe river.

2. Tape together several large sheets of paper or paper bags. Cut a winding or straight river. Make the river the length of the block corner.

3. Lay the river on top of some newspapers, and, together with the children, paint it blue, blue-green, or white, using flat paint brushes.

4. When the river is dry, tape it on the floor in the block area. Find pictures of bridges. Hang them on the wall in the block corner. Make sure the pictures are at the children's eye level.

Activity: Ask the children to imagine that this is really water. Discuss how a car, person, or animal could get across the river. When bridges are mentioned, invite children to start building. If bridges are not mentioned, introduce the idea through a book or the pictures in the block corner. Keep in mind children's individual stages of development. Some children may not be ready to construct bridges, but they can enjoy the river as they pursue their own level of dramatic play. Some children may start with a simple bridge laid across the river. Encourage older children to experiment with more elaborate structures. For example: "Can a boat go under your bridge?" This may lead to elevating the structure. Asking the question "Can a really large, heavy truck cross your bridge?" may lead to wider and stronger structures.

Extensions and variations:

- Play stepping stones. Place make-believe (paper) stones "in the water." Invite the children to cross the river on the stones. This game helps to develop large muscles and coordination.

- Plan a visit to a bridge near the classroom. What does the bridge carry—cars, people, animals, trains? What is the bridge made of—brick, stone, wood, steel?

 to 

The Hoist

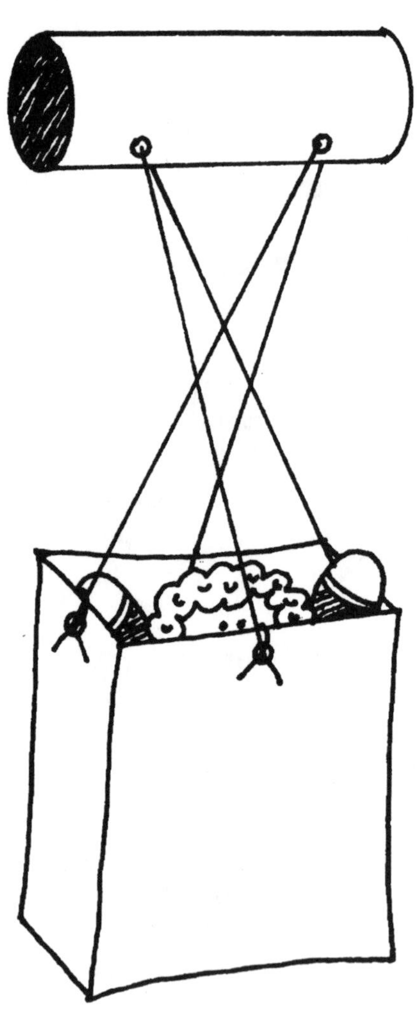

HOME CONNECTION

Encourage parents to take children on an elevator ride. Go up the elevator and walk down the stairs. Explain that machines make work easier for people. What machines make work easier at home?

Purpose: Through block play, children learn about stability and balance and enhance their spatial skills. They acquire the foundations they need to understand length, width, height, and area. Teachers can stimulate block play by providing simple props such as a hoist or elevator to bring people or things to the top of the block buildings. Children in rural settings may be unfamiliar with elevators but may have seen a hoist.

Materials:

toilet paper tube
scissors
paper punch or sharp point
string
small box

Preparation:

1. Punch a hole in 4 sides of a small box from which one end has been removed.

2. Punch holes near the ends of the paper tube. To attach the box, thread the string through the two holes in the tube and tie a knot at each end of the string on the outside of the box.

3. By rolling the string around the tube, you have an "elevator."

Activity: Place the hoist on a shelf in the block corner. The teacher might encourage exploration by saying, "I wonder how the workers would get materials up to such a tall building?" or "I wonder how a person would get to the top of your building?" It may be necessary to show the child how the elevator works. Place a small block or some pegs into the elevator/hoist and demonstrate. Then let the child explore.

Extensions and variations:

- Depending on the age of the children, the teacher might explain the difference between an elevator or lift for people, and a hoist for things.

- If the children have not had experience with an elevator or a hoist, arrange a trip to see either or both of these, if possible.

 to 

Traffic Signs

HOME CONNECTION

Parents are always welcome in the classroom. When they are dropping off or picking up their children, invite the parents to come in and look around. This is a good time to point out the structures that the children have been working on in the block area. Call attention to the signs and labels that have been made for the roads and buildings. Ask the parents to help their children focus on signs in the environment as they walk or ride through town. This will help their children gather ideas for making signs, a first step in early writing.

Purpose: Block play is both structured and open-ended. The blocks are limited in shape and number, but the play itself follows the individual interest and skill of each child. By creating traffic signals and other signs and placing them in the block corner, teachers set the stage for children to develop a sight vocabulary.

Materials:

cardboard	wood sticks
small blocks of wood	drill
markers	glue

Preparation:

1. On sturdy cardboard, in large letters and appropriate colors, create a series of traffic signs and signals, including: Red Light, Yellow Light, Green Light, Stop Sign, Rail Road Crossing, No Passing.

2. Drill holes in the small blocks of wood.

3. Glue each sign to a stick and glue the stick into the small block of wood.

4. Place the signs in the block corner.

Activity: Observe the way children build in the block corner. Listen to their conversations with themselves and other children. If they use cars and make roads, introduce the road signs and give a simple explanation of each.

When children identify what they are building, create a sign for them by writing the name of their building on paper. Use a sheet of thick paper, folded horizontally so that the sign can stand on the floor near the building. Present the sign with a statement: "I thought you might like a sign for your building." Signs might read: The Farm, Our School, The Firehouse, The Castle, The Police Station, The Hospital, The Library. At the end of each day, place the signs in a box or file folder on a shelf that children can reach near the block corner. Children often repeat their buildings or get new ideas from other children. If they ask for the signs, show them how you pick out the sign. After a while, some children will be able to select the sign without help. Some will be ready to read the signs.

If children have not identified what they built, ask if they want a sign and what they want you to write.

Extensions and variations:

- Plan walking trips near the classroom. What signs do you see along the way? What do the children think the signs say? Listen for the different sounds of traffic.

- Read aloud a book with pictures of vehicles. Point out any signs in the book.

 to 

Parking Garage

HOME CONNECTION

Explain to parents they should take advantage of the presence of numbers in the environment. Daily routines and common situations involve opportunities to help children understand the importance of counting and number relationships.

Purpose: When children are freely engaged in block building, they often use small cars and trucks as they build. An alert teacher observes, listens, and supports children's endeavors by introducing props that will expand thinking and problem solving in their play. Selecting a car with dots on the roof and "driving" it into a garage with the corresponding numeral on the top is a way for children to learn matching, counting, and ordering.

Materials:

5 milk cartons
thick colored paper
scissors
clear contact paper (if available)
small cards
black markers
small plastic cars or trucks

Preparation:

1. To make garages, cover the cartons with thick colored paper, then, if available, with clear contact paper.

2. Make number cards: On one side of the card, put dots (for children who have not yet mastered numerals); on the other side, write the corresponding numeral. Use the numbers 1 to 5. Place a number card on top of each garage.

3. Take 5 small plastic cars or trucks and mark 1 dot on top of the first car, 2 dots on the second car, 3 dots on the third car, etc.

Activity: Introduce the activity with a suggestion to the children in the block area: "When the weather is bad, you may need to park your cars in garages. I have some numbered garages and cars. If you like, you can choose from among these." Draw the children's attention to the dots on the cars. Ask the children to count the dots. "How many dots are there? Can you find the garage for this car? Why do you think this car should be parked in this garage? Where do you think this car goes?"

Extensions and variations:

- Have some extra cars and number-and-dot cards ready for children who want to number cars beyond the ones the teacher provides.

- Ask the children to think of other "things-that-go-into-things"—for example, birds and nests, babies in buggies. Have each child draw a picture of her chosen object in its corresponding place. Put the pictures together in book form. Older children will enjoy looking at this book in the future.

 to 

Discovering Equivalence

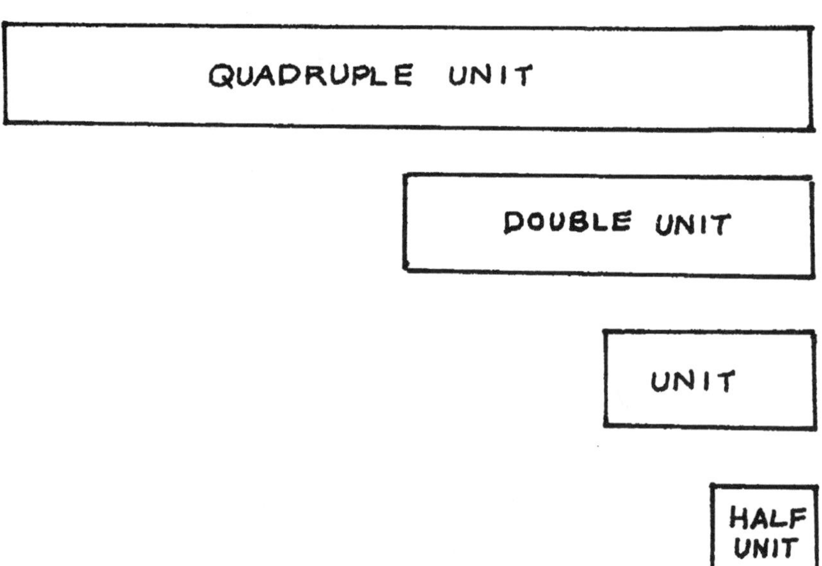

Purpose: This activity encourages children to measure, using blocks as the unit of measurement. Children observe the proportional relationship of one size block to another and become exposed to mathematical terms.

Materials: a chart
classroom blocks: half unit blocks, unit blocks, double unit, and quads

The unit is a rectangle (3.5 x 7 x 14 cm.).
The half unit is square (3.5 x 7 x 7 cm.).
The double unit block is a rectangle (3.5 x 7 x 28 cm.).
The quadruple unit is a rectangle (3.5 x 7 x 56 cm.).

Activity: As children are building, they usually discover *on their own* equivalency among the different sized blocks. For example, they are able to use 2 unit blocks to substitute for 1 double unit block. The teacher can use this opportunity to acquaint children with mathematical terminology by using the word *equivalent*: "Maria, I see you have found that two units are equivalent to (the same length as) one double unit. Good for you! Let's write this on a chart." " Emil, you have been using the double units. How many did you need to match a quad? Yes—2 doubles. I wonder how many units you would need to be the equivalent of a quad. Yes—4 units. Let's draw pictures of what you discovered on the chart."

When a child builds vertically or horizontally, a rope or string may be used to measure the height or length of the structure. Suggest the children try measuring a table's length, height of chairs from floor, etc.

Extensions and variations:

- At a parents' meeting, have them use the blocks to build as they wish.
- Prepare a display, showing how valuable blocks are to teach mathematical concepts.
- Show how blocks are placed on the shelves so that children can recognize sizes and can have a classification activity by putting them away.

 to 

Inclined Planes

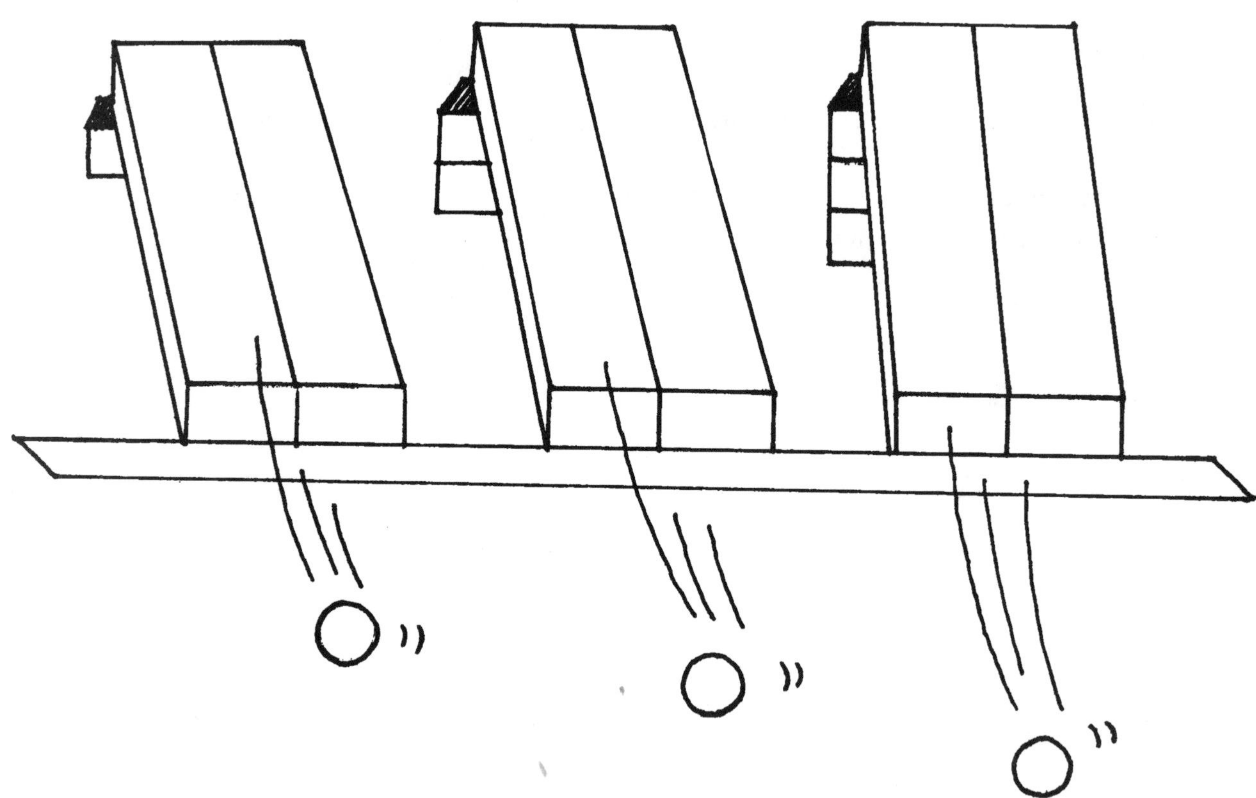

Purpose: This activity is designed to show the effect of inclined planes on speed and distance. It lays a foundation for children to become familiar with the scientific investigation processes of predicting, experimenting, observing, discovering, describing, comparing, inferring, classifying, and communicating. Encourage girls' and boys' interest in science by conducting simple active experiments.

Materials:

- 6 unit blocks
- 6 quadruple unit blocks
- 3 small hard balls
- masking tape
- paper dots

Preparation:

1. This is an activity for groups of 3 children at one time. Explain to the group that each child will have a turn being a scientist and experimenting with these materials.

2. Find a spacious area to conduct this experiment, such as a hallway, a paved smooth surface outdoors, or a gym. The teacher and children build 3 ramps of varying heights and then see how far the same ball travels after it rolls down them. The steeper the incline, the farther the ball goes.

3. To build the ramps, each child gets 2 quadruple unit blocks and either 1, 2, or 3 unit blocks. Each ramp will be the width of 2 quadruple blocks (or long boards). The height of the ramp is determined by the number of unit blocks: the first 2 quadruple blocks will be placed on top of 1 unit block; the next 2 will be placed on 2 unit blocks; and the next 2 will be placed on 3 unit blocks. Place a strip of masking tape along the floor so that the ends of the ramps will line up and the ball will always travel from the same place. Point out that since this is a science experiment, it is important that all the ramps end at the strip of masking tape.

Activity: When the ramps are built, ask each child to predict how far the ball will roll. Have each child go to the spot where she predicts the ball will stop and mark the spot with a large dot. Explain to the children that in this experiment, they cannot throw the ball; they must place the ball on the top of the ramp and just let go.

Children should experiment with their own ramps and balls a few times. After they have done so, ask some questions such as, "Did the ball go farther than you predicted, or not? Which ball rolled the farthest? Which ball stopped closest to the ramp?"

At this point, have the children take turns with each ramp. Then ask, "Why do you think the ball rolled farther on one ramp than another? Did the ball roll faster on any ramp?" Eventually, help the children to understand that the higher the ramp, the faster and farther the ball will roll.

Extensions and variations:

- Explain that scientists document their observations. Make a chart with the children to document their experiment.

- Give children turns rolling a ball down the slide on the playground.

- Make a ramp outdoors. Using the ramp, experiment with balls of differing sizes and weight. What conclusions can the children draw from their observations?

MUSIC

 to 

HOME CONNECTION

Suggest that parents and children go on a "sound search" around their homes. They can have fun shaking household objects and testing for vibrations.

Purpose: This experiment is designed to help children differentiate various sounds. It is an auditory matching exercise, in which children find pairs of the same sound. Children refine auditory skills as they attend to subtle distinctions in sound.

Materials:
- buttons
- seeds
- paper clips
- small plastic containers with lids (empty film canisters or vitamin containers)

Preparation:
1. In each of 2 identical containers, place an equal amount of seeds.
2. In each of 2 identical containers, place the same number of same-sized buttons.
3. In each of 2 identical containers, place the same number of same-sized paper clips.
4. Put lids on all the containers.

Activity: In a small group of 3, have the children experiment with shaking each of the 6 sound cans. Ask, "Do all the cans sound alike?" They may find that some do and some don't. Then ask them to try to find those that sound alike. When children match a pair, ask them to describe the sounds. Also ask what they think is making the sounds.

Extensions and variations:
- Add or take away some of the contents of the containers. Have the children shake the cans. Ask, "How does this change the sound? What would happen if we mixed the contents? Could we still make a pair?"
- Sound cans can be used to create rhythmic patterns or shake out a song.

Maracas

 to 

Purpose: Maracas are percussion instruments. Playing maracas provides an opportunity for children to experience sequencing rhythmic patterns. The process of making and playing maracas increases a child's fine motor development. With careful teacher guidance, children discover a variety of pitches and compare them. Children shake out patterns using their maracas.

HOME CONNECTION

Parents, teach your child a song that you sang when you were your child's age.

Materials:

- toilet paper tubes
- aluminum foil
- tempera paint
- thick paper
- rubber bands
- ribbons, yarn
- crepe paper streamers
- seeds, pebbles, and bottle caps

Preparation:

1. The children paint the exterior of the paper tubes.

2. When the paint is dry, the children cover one end of the paper tube with aluminum foil or thick paper secured with a rubber band. Younger children should be assisted by adult helpers.

3. They fill the paper tube with a handful of seeds, pebbles, or bottle caps.

4. The opened end is then secured as in Step 2.

5. Children can decorate the outside of the paper tube with crepe paper streamers, ribbons, or yarn.

Activity: In a small or large group, children sit in a circle and take turns establishing a rhythm, which the group then follows. For example, use the rhythm of each child's name: Jo-nas—2 beats; El-e-na—3 beats. Ask the children to guess how the sound is made. Have them experiment shaking their maracas at different rates—fast, slow, medium. Ask what sound is made when the maraca is rolled or tapped.

Extensions and variations:

- Sing or play a song, using the maracas to keep time.

- Play music on a record or tape and have the children parade around the room, keeping the beat of the music.

- Ask older children to describe the pattern. For example: beat, beat, rest, beat, beat, rest.

- Make a tambourine. Use crayons, paint, and paper to decorate two paper plates. Select pebbles, bottle caps, or seeds, and place a handful on one plate. Staple the plates together.

Kazoo

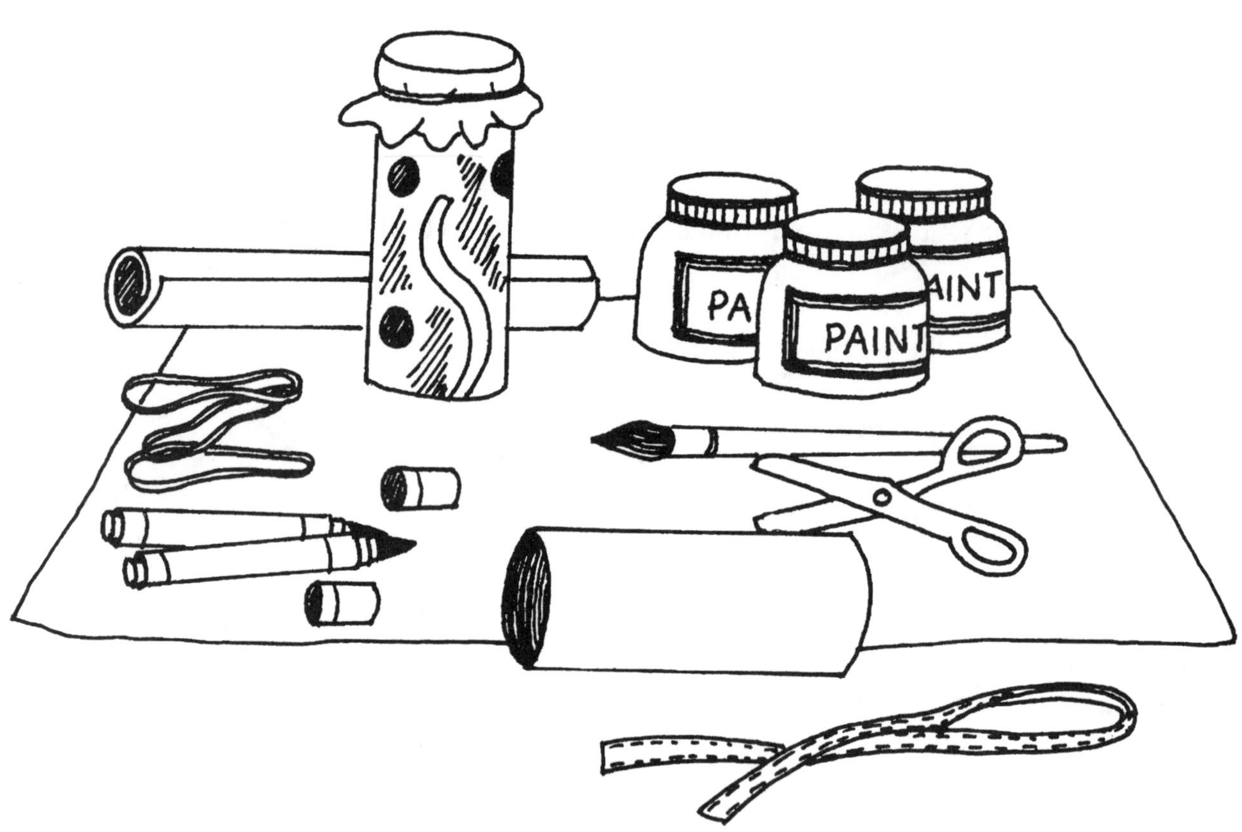

HOME CONNECTION

Invite parents to the class to share their musical talents, such as singing or playing an instrument. In this way, parents model an enjoyment of music for children.

Purpose: Sound is vibration. Making a kazoo is a creative way for children to discover how air vibrates through wax paper to make high and low pitches. Besides gaining personal satisfaction and pleasure by humming out a favorite song, children will begin to understand that lower pitches vibrate slower and higher pitches vibrate faster.

Materials:

- toilet paper tubes
- tempera paint
- brushes
- decorative paper
- glue
- wax paper
- rubber bands
- scissors
- markers

Preparation:

1. Encourage each child to decorate a paper tube. Provide decorative paper, markers, and paint.

2. Make a kazoo by fastening a piece of wax paper over one end of the tube. Use a rubber band to secure the wax paper. Younger children may need help. Older children should be encouraged to complete this step independently.

Activity: Have the children hum into the kazoo. Try humming softly. Then try humming loudly. Make high sounds, then low sounds. Explore a variety of ways to make the kazoo vibrate. Play a song as a group. Ask for volunteers to play a "solo."

Extensions and variations:

- Play music on a record player or tape recorder and have the children parade around the room humming on their kazoos to the beat of the music.

- In a small group, ask older children to hum out a pitch pattern. Then have the other children guess the pitch pattern. For example, the pattern could be: high pitch, low pitch, high pitch, low pitch.

 to 

Wooden Harps

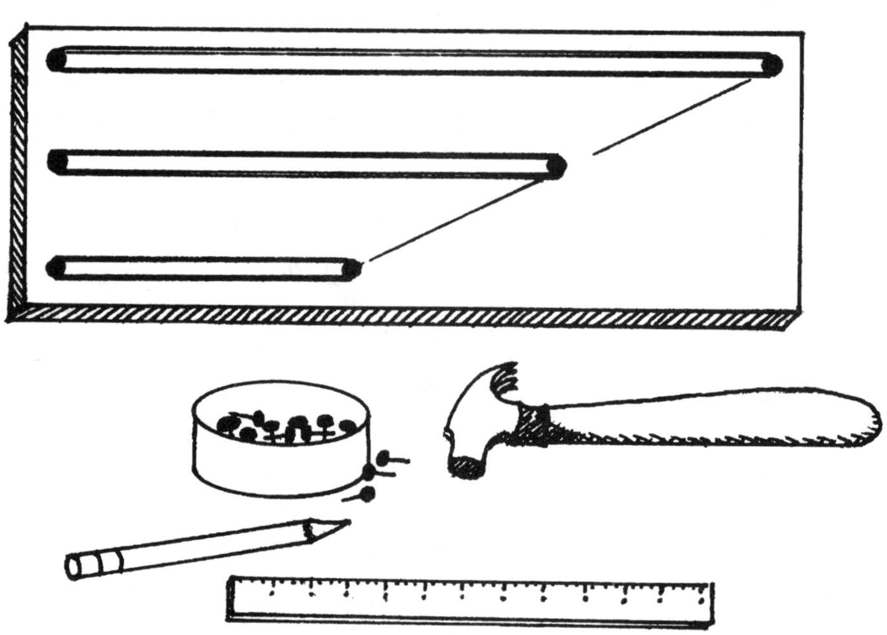

Purpose: This activity is designed to encourage children to become aware of sound and to experiment with musical instruments. Children are alert to the sounds around them and in the outdoor environment.

HOME CONNECTION

Suggest that families form an informal "family band" using handmade instruments. Hold a "sing along" at school in the evening, and invite families to come and sing and play instruments.

Materials:

- wood
- rubber bands
- nails
- markers
- hammer

Preparation:

1. Use a piece of flat wood, long enough to stretch out 3 different sizes of rubber bands. Mark the board so that children can hammer 3 evenly spaced nails vertically along the left side of the board. On the right side, starting from the top, mark a diagonal line so that the second and third nails will be opposite the left side but at shorter distances. See illustration.

Activity: The children hammer in the nails and stretch the rubber bands across them. They then strum on their harps. Suggest that they hold the back of the harps against their ears while strumming them. This way the sound will be more intense. Encourage the children to experiment with which rubber band makes the highest sound and which makes the lowest sound.

Extensions and variations:

- Make lid vibrations: Collect jar lids and many sizes of rubber bands. Stretch rubber bands around the lids. Pluck the rubber bands and listen to the different sounds. Do larger lids make different sounds than smaller lids? Hold rubber bands in place with tape. What is the effect on the sound?

- Fill several glass containers with different amounts of water. Have small groups of children take turns tapping each with a stick. Is the sound the same? What makes the sound different? If the container is without water, will it make a sound?

- Have the children go on a sound walk around the center or outdoors. If possible, record the sounds for the children to identify the next day. If no recorder is available, make a chart with visual representations of the object that makes the sound—a picture of a garbage truck, a picture of a bird—and have the children try to recreate the sounds.

Box Banjo

to

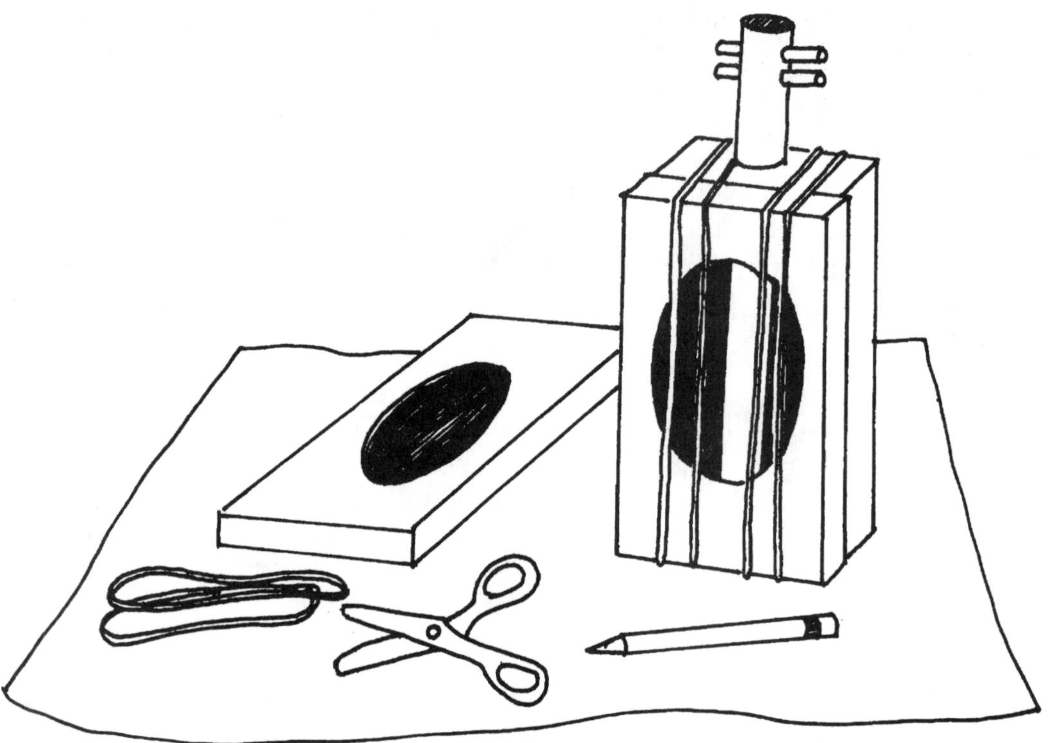

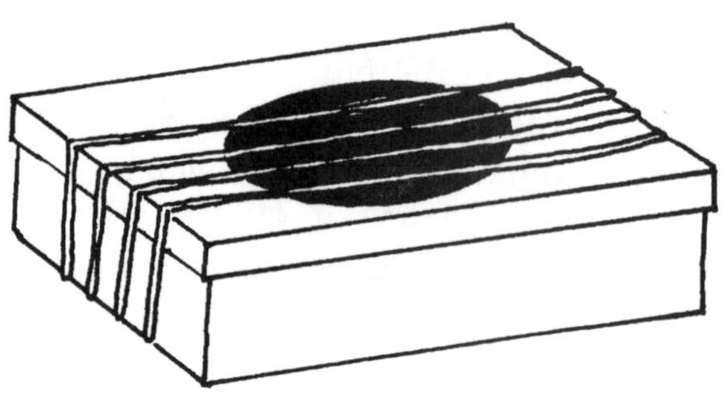

HOME CONNECTION

Suggest that parents discuss traditional instruments with their children and the kinds of folk songs they learned as children.

Purpose: Young children are natural music makers. Children can make and play banjos using boxes and rubber bands. Making and playing instruments fosters a child's basic understanding of vibration, pitch, and tone. The teacher elicits critical thinking skills by asking children to notice higher and lower pitches. Through a process of questioning, discussing, and comparing sounds, children discover that shorter rubber bands produce a higher pitch, whereas longer rubber bands produce a lower pitch.

Materials:

shoe box with lid
large rubber bands
scissors
cardboard tube—optional
sticks or pencils—optional

Preparation:

1. Ask volunteer parents to make 2 or 3 box banjos for the class. Using scissors, cut the oval opening in the center of the lid of the box.

2. Place the lid on the box and stretch rubber bands across the opening of the box. The rubber bands should be about an inch apart.

3. A long cardboard tube and pencils or sticks can be optionally added.

Activity: In a small group, let each child explore the box banjos, gently plucking the rubber bands over the hole. Ask the children what they notice about the sound as they play the banjo. Do all rubber bands make the same sounds? Can any conclusions be drawn regarding the different tones? How can the sound be changed?

Extensions and variations:

- Ask each child to work with a partner to find tones that sound alike and different on their box banjos.

- Establish various rhythms for children to follow. For example, plunk, plunk, rest, plunk, plunk, rest. Suggest that rhythms are patterns of sounds. Have the children make up their own patterns and play for each other.

- Sing a song and accompany it on the box banjo.

REFERENCES

Adams, L. & Garlick (eds.). (1979). Ideas that work with young children, Vol. 2. Washington, DC: National Association for the Education of Young Children.

Allen, D. (1988). Science demonstrations for the elementary classroom. New York: Parker.

Baratta-Lorton, M. (1972). Workjobs: Activity-centered learning for early childhood education. Reading, MA: Addison-Wesley.

Bruno, J. (1994). Hands-on math: Manipulative activities for the k-1 classroom. Cypress, CA: Creative Teaching Press.

Burca, R. and Rothschild, J. (1974). The activity shuttle. New York: New York University.

Burns, M. (1992). About teaching mathematics: A k-8 resource. New York: Math Solutions Publications.

Cherry, C. (1972). Creative art for the developing child: A teacher's handbook for early childhood education. Belmont, CA: Fearnon

Coughlin, P.A., Hansen, K.A., Heller, D., Kauffman, R.K., Rothschild Stolberg, J., and Walsh, K.B. (1997). Creating child-centered classrooms: 3-5 year olds. Washington, DC: Children's Resources International.

Eliason, C.F. & Jenkins, L.T. (1981). A practical guide to early childhood curriculum (2nd ed.). St. Louis, MO: The C.V. Mosby Company.

Gene-Holt, B. (1977). Science with young children. Washington, DC: National Association for the Education of Young Children.

Green, M.D. (1995). Teaching from cupboards & closets: Integrated learning activities for young children. Glenview, IL: GoodYearBooks.

Harlan, J.D. & Jenkins, M.S. (1996). Science experiences for the early childhood years: An integrated approach (6th ed.). Englewood Cliffs, NJ: Merrill.

Hirsch, E.S. (ed.). (1984). The block book. Washington, DC: National Association for the Education of Young Children.

Hymes, J. (1981). Teaching the child under six (3rd ed.). Columbus, OH: Charles E. Merrill.

Johnson, V. (1994). Hands-on math: Manipulative activities for the k-1 classroom. Cypress, CA: Creative Teaching Press.

Jones, C. (1988). Parents are teachers too. Charlotte, VT: Williamson Publishing Co.

Kohl, M. (1994). Preschool art: It's the process, not the product. Beltsville, MD: Gryphon House.

Kranzer, H. (1967). Nursery & kindergarten science activities. Jenkintown, PA: Prime-Ed Company.

Levenson, E. (1985). Teaching children about science: Ideas and activities every teacher and parent can use. Englewood Cliffs, NJ: Prentice-Hall.

Mayesky, M. Neuman, D., & Wlodkowski, R.J. (1980). Creative activities for young children (2nd ed.). Albany, NY: Delmar.

Nickelsburg, J. (1976). Nature activities for early childhood. Reading, MA: Addison Wesley.

Olshansky, B. (1990). Portfolio of illustrated step-by-step art projects for young children. West Nyack, NY: The Center for Applied Research in Education.

Rasmussen, M. (1965). Young children and science. Washington, DC: Association for Childhood Education International.

Schickedanz, J.A., York, M.E., Stewart, I.S., & White, D. (1977). Strategies for teaching young children. Englewood Cliffs, NJ: Prentice-Hall.

Schwartz, J. (1966). Science grades k-2. New York: Board of Education.

Seefeldt, C. & Barbour, N. (1990). Early childhood education: An introduction (2nd ed.). New York: Merrill.

Sprung, B., Froschl, M., & Campbell, P. (1985). What will happen if. New York: Educational Equity Concepts, Inc.

Tilgner, L. (1988). Let's grow!: 72 Gardening adventures with children. Pownel, VT: Storey Communications.

VanCleave, J. (1991). Janice VanCleave's earth science for every kid: 101 Easy experiments that really work. New York: John Wiley & Sons.

Walton, J. (1974). Logical-mathematical thinking and the preschool classroom. College Park, MD: Head Start Regional Resource and Training Center.

Williams, R.A., Rockwell, R.E., & Sherwood, E.A. (1987). Mudpies to magnets: A preschool science curriculum. Mt. Rainier, MD: Gryphon House.

Wood, C. (1994). Yardsticks: Children in the classroom ages 4-12. Greenfield, MA: Northeast Foundation for Children.

Zaslavsky, C. (1979). Preparing young children for math. New York: Schocken Books.

Creating Child-Centered Classroom Series

Creating Child-Centered Classrooms: 3-5 Year Olds

Helps teachers create active learning environments for preschool-age children, individualize teaching, and involve families in the program. Teachers learn observation techniques to teach to the strengths, interests, and needs of each child.

Creating Child-Centered Materials

Assists educators in designing and making their own classroom materials for active exploration. Each activity includes a "home connection" that links the child's family to the classroom learning experiences. Easy-to-follow directions allow teachers to create activities from recycled and natural materials for math, science and language arts.

Creating Inclusive Classrooms

Provides the research base, practical methods and real-world case studies that guide and support teachers through issues such as family partnerships, IEP development, and adapting the classroom environment.

Making a Difference: A Parent's Guide to Advocacy and Community Action

Provides practical advice to help parents become effective advocates in their school and communities. Step-by-step directions and real-life stories of successful advocates are interwoven to guide readers through the process of advocacy.

For more information, contact:

Children's Resources International
5039 Connecticut Ave., NW
Suite One
Washington, DC 20008
phone: 202-363-9002
fax: 202-363-9550
info@crinter.com
www.childrensresources.org

Creating Child-Centered Programs for Infants and Toddlers

Provides the research base that supports the need for quality programs. It shows caregivers how to design a safe, healthy, and responsive environment for infants and toddlers; how to support young children's learning; and how to staff and evaluate a child-centered program for infants and toddlers.

Learning Activities for Infants and Toddlers: An Easy Guide for Everyday Use

Offers caregivers more than 100 hands-on, developmentally appropriate activities that caregivers can incorporate into the child's day. Each activity includes a purpose, list of materials, and simple steps for preparation. In addition, each activity provides a "home connection," to involve parents and extend the activity at home.

Creating Child-Centered Classrooms: 6-7 Year Olds

Provides teachers with lessons, suggestions for extending activities, assessment strategies and forms, thematic curriculum webs, and complete resource and reference lists. This volume presents four powerful themes that unify program concepts and goals: Communication, Caring, Community, and Connections.

Creating Child-Centered Classrooms: 8-10 Year Olds

Presents a unique blend of current, exemplary educational practices and sound theory to address the educational needs of children in the later early childhood years. It addresses the content areas of mathematics, literacy, social studies, science, and the visual arts.

Education and The Culture of Democracy

Explains the link between democracy and early childhood practice. This book contends that there are subtle, yet effective teaching techniques that encourage democracy: choice, individualism, creativity, equality, respect for differences, and appreciation of individuals' needs while maintaining the balance for the greater good of the group.